On The Outside Looking In

By Kathy Carniero

Surviving
The Blindside
of Addiction

On The Outside Looking In

Surviving the Blind Side of Addiction

Kathy Carniero

Published by Live Love Learn Books Publishing

LIVE
L⩗VE
LEARN
BOOKS
PUBLISHING

LiveLoveLearnBooks.com

On the Outside Looking In
Original cover design by Dana Pierson
Cover design by Cindy Shtevi
Tattoo designed by: Scott Burleson, Ben Powell,
and Adam Belial.
Photographer: Kathy Lucca

Printed in the United States of America
Library Of Congress Control Number: 2014920994

ISBN-10: 099030440X
ISBN-13: 978-0-9903044-0-1

Dedication

I dedicate this book to my family, friends and everyone
that has been blindsided by addiction.

Table of Contents

"I'm on the outside looking in
I believe the devil has pulled you in
With this addiction you are lost
Without a fight you will pay the cost
God is on your side
But it is up to you to decide
The angels watched over you today
But tomorrow you will have to lead the way
I'm on the outside looking in
I believe you have the strength within
Do not let the addiction steal your heart
You will be left broken and ripped apart
With help you can be strong
I believe you can live forever long
I'm on the outside looking in
This battle I know you can win"

<u>Introduction</u>

"I have learned that you cannot change an addict, but merely learn how to cope with their addiction, until they are ready to change for themselves."

If you're reading this you have either experienced or you're currently experiencing the grueling pain, personal guilt, helplessness, stress, anger and anxiety with living on the blind side of someone else's addiction. You are not alone in this whirl wind of a journey. I have been where you are. I know how the hurt and pain can consume your whole life. I watched first-hand how addiction destroys. I know how hard it is to watch someone you love kill them self slowly and nothing you do will make them stop. The sleepless nights you have endured worried and sickened by this addiction. You're not alone. I also know how angry and frustrated you are with your addict and how you may struggle with your own happiness. These feelings we feel are real and normal. We are scared and sad for our loved ones. We know the truth even though it is hard to accept. The truth is that we cannot save them unless they are ready to save themselves.

I do not think we will ever truly understand addiction, but I do know firsthand that sharing my story, educating myself and hearing the stories from addicts has helped me tremendously get a grasp on this sickness. I have experienced the blind side of alcohol and crystal meth addiction.

I cannot write about how an addict truly feels or what they

have been through because I have never been in their shoes. You will hear the voices and hearts from addicts and me, through our journeys of addiction.

I am going to refer to your loved ones and mine as an "addict." It took me a long time to come to the realization that this was the name for my loved one, until I did my research and educated myself. I learned that my loved one fell under almost every category of an addict, and (like the denial of an addict) it was also a part of my own denial that I refused to accept. I learned that it was entirely up to them to stand up to their addiction to turn it all around.

People say that the addicts are the ones who suffer and are victimized the most, as agreed they are, but then there is the family, friends, and loved ones who are also affected. We as non addicts are lied to, taken advantage of, stolen from, hurt, sad, confused, defeated, and angry.

Unless you have experienced addiction for yourself first hand then you're often left in the dark with what you are up against.

At first you don't see it happening, then all of sudden you're watching your loved one slowly killing themselves and all their worth due to their addiction. You watch helplessly as you ask yourself what to do? How did this happen? What can I do to save this person from themselves? When and how did it get so bad? Why won't they listen to me? Why won't they get help? What happened in their life that they felt so helpless they turned to drugs/alcohol to try to numb their pain? You look at the addict in your life in dismay and disbelief that they have become everything you have raised them not to be; or your parent that has taught you not to drink or do drugs, loses their life to addiction and does not follow through with their own teachings. You're in shock and disgusted with yourself that you cannot help them or change them. You neglect your own life and focus all your energy on them in hopes they will get better. You hold on until the bitter end.

Most of the time your questions will go unanswered and I think that is one of the hardest parts of living with someone else's addiction. You end up beating yourself up mentally trying to find the answers, when in reality the addict using doesn't even have the answers.

What I have experienced in my life is that most people with an addiction have been through a few traumatic events, and or struggles. Some have struggled through heart breaking divorces, loss of their loved ones, abuse as a child or as an adult, sexual abuse, mental abuse, physical abuse, issues with self-worth and self-esteem, some dabbled into drugs for experimenting and got hooked, and some may just be in a bad place in their life with work or personal issues leaving them feeling helpless and depressed. Many addicts may have underlining mental disorders that have gone undiagnosed or have not been treated properly- such as anxiety, depression, bipolar disorder, obsessive compulsive disorder, multiple personality disorder, anger issues, and emotional disorders. I have also noticed a lot of addicts are afraid to face the reality of their lives and their addictions. Many addicts do not have the knowledge or know the proper way to deal with the ups and downs of life. This results in them using drugs/alcohol to escape their reality and suppress their feelings.

Just as we do not understand the addict's life, the addict will never understand what we have gone through while trying to cope and understand their addiction.

Family and friends deal with someone else's addiction in so many different ways. There are the angry and confused ones who do not know what to do at all and become depressed themselves because they don't know what they can do to help. Then there are the ones who turn the other way and try to believe it is not happening and go on with their everyday business wondering in the back of their mind if this addict will ever get the help they need and deserve. Then there are the ones like me who will go to the extreme in trying everything in their man power to try to help their addict realize their addiction and try to save them from themselves. There is no right or wrong way to deal with someone's addiction and we cannot judge the way someone reacts and deals with this sickness.

Addiction is not something anyone should feel embarrassed or ashamed about. The thing about addiction is that the addict can change this sickness around for the better and live a better and happier life.

"Addicts are not bad people, they are lost in a world of chaos and even though not all of them will choose to be saved from their addiction I believe many of them will."

Dear Mom,

There are so many things I wished I had the chance to tell you before you passed. You were an excellent mother, always teaching me how to be proper and how to show my manners growing up. You taught me how to "sit like a lady" and how to chew with my mouth closed. You helped me through my struggles as a teen and always gave me great advice. You were so strong willed and had a heart of gold. I know the struggles you went through with me. Doing everything you could have done in your power to help me. I wish I had the chance to tell you how much I love you and that the life I chose to live was not your fault. I did listen to your guidance and your words of wisdom even though I chose the wrong path in life. If I knew what this life would have done to me and to you I would have done things so differently. You were a great mother and my inspiration. I had my own troubles and demons within me. I pray you did not live the last of your days feeling guilty for not being able to help me. I thought at that time the drugs were in control and I wasn't ready. I struggle with that every day, but I cannot change the past. You did everything right for me, loved me when no one did, believed in me when everyone turned their back on me. I am sorry for the chaos I caused in your life; I was confused and selfish at that time. I was ashamed of what I had become and even though you told me you forgave me I couldn't face you. I let you down and I wish now I could have thanked you for the life you gave me and the things you taught me. I would have made you proud by now, I know I would have. I am beating my

addiction and I now face my fears with strength and the knowledge

that I can get through anything. I will no longer let a drug rule my

life and steal away my feelings and hope. I love you

unconditionally and even though you are not here to read this

letter I know you're around me. I can feel your love and

encouragements every day. Thank you for being my brave mother;

you are now my guardian angel.

Love your daughter,

Amy Heggiens

In recovery from crack/cocaine

Although it is hard and most of us find ourselves doing so, we should not label an addict. Using terms like "crack head" "alcoholic" "junkie" "meth head" "Ice princess" "lush" "tweaker" "loser" "dopy" and many more I am sure you can add. Doing this is a sad way of saying someone is dying from their sickness.

We may not like their lifestyle, the choices they made and what they are doing, but just like you and me these people once had a future and a life filled with happiness. They experienced love and knew what it meant. They once had hope. Somewhere along the way addiction robbed them of everything they ever had and dreamed of. It corrupted their heart and soul.

1

<u>Addiction</u>

"Addiction does not act alone. Addiction forms the addict, and the addict's personality. Without addiction we would not have addicts."

When you hear the word "addiction" what is the first thought that comes to mind? I did a small survey about what people thought of when they heard the word addiction. The responses that I got had to do with the emotional part of addiction. Some responses from non addicts were they wanted to know how to help the addict, some related it to drugs and alcohol. Some compared addiction to lost souls and a fight to gain their lives back. Some had feelings of sadness, hopelessness, sorrow, and a hope for recovery for an addict.

Fear. That is the only word to describe how I feel about sobriety. Fear is killing me. Fear is holding me back from recovery. I fear not having my drug. I fear my inner self. I fear for what sober life is going to be like. I fear to help myself. I feel like a coward. I know what I need to do, but I just cannot find the courage. I fear change. I fear my feelings. I fear the ability to face myself and my addiction.
Joe Dunns
A struggling addict.

There is more to addiction than just the emotional part of it.

It is a physical and mental state of being enslaved to a habit that is psychologically and physically habit forming. It is also the compulsive and uncontrolled dependency on a substance. (Coon. *et al*, p. 34).

The addict is the one who becomes enslaved to the addictions' curse. The addict may also show signs of an addictive personality. They use in a compulsive and uncontrolled manner in the attempt to cope with their pain and anxiety (p. 34).

When people say something is "habit forming," what I think they really need to say is if you use uncontrollably you *will* become an addict.

The word addiction originated in 1595, a Latin word meaning "a giving over, surrender" (Mifflin, 2002).

Addiction has been around for centuries and centuries. Each century dealt with addiction in their own ways according to their knowledge and morals. The Egyptians flogged addicts and drunkards to get rid of them. The Romans created a god for wine named Bacchus. The Turks way of curing addiction was to pour molten lead down the throats of the addicts. The Greeks would put amethyst stone in their drinking cups and crush them up and put it in their wine to ward off addiction to alcohol.

Alexander, the great King of Macedonia in 350 B.C was the

first well known addict. After addiction to alcohol became a part of his life he drank himself to death at 33.

Over six million children in America live with at least one parent that has a drug/alcohol addiction.

"Addiction itself has not changed, what has changed though is our knowledge, our resources and the way we approach and handle this sickness"

<u>Symptoms of addiction</u>

There are many signs that go along with an addicted person. Some signs may be hard to see especially if the person is trying to hide their addiction. Without the knowledge of these signs it may be harder to relate their behavior with an addiction. Some signs can be from other situations in life so watch carefully before you make assumptions that someone is an addict. Here are some symptoms you may see in an addict.

- Resentful attitude towards their friends and family
- Risky behavior that is out of character
- Aggressive behavior or passiveness
- Mood swings
- Physical symptoms including weight gain or weight loss,
- Being addicted to other drugs, legal or illegal
- Nervous twitches or ticks
- Change in personal hygiene
- Reactive behavior instead of proactive behavior
- Always feeling overwhelmed
- Not trusting anyone
- Low self-esteem, never feeling good enough
- Depression
- Anxiety
- Lethargy
- Their skin color may be yellowish
- Their face can be sunken in
- Skin broken out in sores
- Different body odors
- Becoming withdrawn from themselves and others
- Erratic behavior
- Obvious drug or alcohol use

You may notice different symptoms in the addict that is in your life. In my opinion never ignore these types of symptoms. The addict probably does not even notice if they are showing signs of their addiction, or they simply refuse to acknowledge them, especially if they are still in the denial stage.

I remember when I first noticed my dad's symptoms. At first it was his lack of hygiene and appearance; I noticed that right away. He was a man who always made sure his hair was freshly cut, combed and face was clean. When his addiction set in he ignored these things. I noticed he stumbled more and was less coordinated. He also always looked tired and drained. His eyes looked red and he always seemed a little confused. I started to notice broken blood vessels in his face and a yellow tint to his skin. He also had a very strange smell to him too. Like the alcohol was seeping out of all his pores but it smelled different? His behavior quickly changed; he became less motivated in work, he began to make excuses so he would not have to involve himself in family functions, he would become very defensive if questioned about his drinking and his spirit was down.

When I would tell him about how I noticed these symptoms he would deny them. Telling me "no" that this was not true, "I do not do that" or "I do not smell funny", or telling me I did not know what I was talking about, making me then second guess myself. Was I really seeing these signs or smelling this smell? I knew I was, but I did not see how he could not see it. Actually he did know it, but the more he told himself these symptoms were not there the more he could believe himself when he said he did not have a problem.

There are 3 types of drinkers/drug users:

1) A Social drinker/user

They seem to use only socially; occasionally having a drink or 2 or a "once in a while hit off of a joint" or a "bump". A social user can easily become addicted with enough use.

2) A Hard Drinker/Drug User

This drinker or drug user appears to be an addict at first. With this user they can stop without aide if negative consequences happen due to their use. Example: A man gets a DWI one night realizes his drinking has caused him conflict. He stops drinking and focuses more on his life.

3) Real Alcoholic/Drug Addict

This drinker or drug user may have periods of abstinence with heavy binges in between or is a continuous user with no will power to stop no matter the effects it has on them, their loved ones and their personal life. The "real" alcoholic/drug user drinks for an underlying reason, as opposed to just "having fun". No matter the negative consequences it has in their life, they will progressively get worse, destroying their hopes and dreams for themselves and their loved ones.

(Lee, 2007 p. 6).

Addiction can be with anything

I believe everyone has some sort of addicted personality in them. Some handle it better than others with self-control, education or simply knowing their own boundaries. Addiction can be with anything you can mentally, physically, or chemically become addicted to.

Other addictions besides drugs and alcohol can be with caffeine, food, gambling, sex, social media, sleeping, and nicotine. Not only can a person get addicted to a substance they can also get addicted to the lifestyle of being an addict. This lifestyle can include:

- Lack of responsibilities
- The freedom of not having a real job
- The party atmosphere
- Having an excuse of why they are not productive
- Not having to worry about their repercussions
- Not dealing with their children
- Being free from paying bills
- Not taking responsibility for their feelings
- Not dealing with life in general
- Not being a part of real society

I have an addiction to caffeine, mainly Starbucks coffee. As crazy as this sounds, it is true. The moment I wake up I have to have coffee or I get a terrible headache. I have to drink up to 3 cups of coffee before I can even feel the effects of it. Everyday around 3 o'clock I start to get a bad headache from not having caffeine. I cannot get away with a small cup of coffee I have to get more than two shots of espresso in my drink or else it's pointless. If I cannot get away from work to get a Starbucks I usually will have someone go get it for me. I spend almost 50$ a week on this addiction. Sometimes I will go twice a day, morning and afternoon. Many times my tolerance to caffeine gets so high I cannot even feel the effects of a triple espresso. I will then try to stay away from espresso for a few days while trying to get my tolerance down. Normally within those few days I experience headaches and agitation. I will still drink my morning coffee though.

My caffeine addiction is similar to a drug or alcohol addiction. Even though my addiction does not get me high, or drunk I still have the cravings, my tolerance is built up, I will spend more money on coffee than any other beverage, I have withdrawal symptoms, I think about it constantly, and my internal body is addicted as well as my mind. I find myself trying to talk myself out of getting coffee throughout the day. Most of the time I give in, then I feel guilty, just like an addict does after they have used. Susan McDonald

I became addicted to my addicts addiction. I tried to justify my addiction to myself by saying "How can I just sit there and watch them slowly kill themselves and do nothing about it?" My addiction took a toll on my family life and my personal life. I soon realized that my intervening and obsession didn't work and sometimes made situations worse. I was told numerous times by my husband, friends and family that I could not control if they lived or died.

I would not admit I had an addiction to their addiction. It was too hard to face my own reality. Then I started to think of how hard it must be for an addict to admit they have an addiction. My addiction consumed everything I did, just like a drug addiction or alcohol addiction does. The only difference with mine is that a substance was not controlling me. I lived and breathed their addiction every day. I wanted to know everything, what they were doing, why they were doing it, who they were with, what their plans were short term and long term, what they were thinking, what they ate that day, when they went to sleep, if they slept good or not. I wanted to be a fly on their wall. I tried to read every book and research everything that had to do with addiction to try to understand their thinking. I did this because I was so scared of losing them I thought if I could have control of their every move, and know everything, I could save them. In reality though, that does not happen with an addict. The more you try to "control them" or try to figure out what they are doing all the time, they become more withdrawn because they are trying to keep their addiction private. The more they would withdraw themselves from me the more I became addicted to trying to help them. I was losing them to their addiction from my addiction of trying to save them.

At that time in my life I did not know if I was doing the right thing by always trying to come up with ways to talk about the addiction and trying to make the addict realize the situation. It was getting out of hand. This resulted in arguments, not speaking at all, the binges getting worse, destroying any relationship that was left, and me being upset all the time. I still don't know if my actions would have changed anything; if I had just let it be and let the sickness take its course, in hopes they would change on their own. I still ask myself, if I had not been so overbearing would they have changed? Did I push them further away? Or if I would have just stepped back and watched as they threw their life away knowing deep down inside they truly did not want to be this way, would I feel better? But when you love someone so much I believe you simply cannot just sit and watch them throw their lives away and die a slow painful death. I call it suicide by addiction. You're watching them drown in their own sorrow and they are so helpless with their actions and emotions.

There are so many mixed feelings here when it comes to trying to help an addict. I don't think there is really a right or wrong way of intervening, for every situation and addict is different. I do believe though that showing your love and never giving up does have an impact. They are listening to what we are saying, but it is them who have to decide if they are going to accept the reality or not.

Anyone can be an Addict

The scary part about addiction is that it can happen to anyone. Age, race, sex, religion, moms, dads, kids, teenagers, sisters, brothers, friends, co-workers, neighbors, aunts, uncles, cousins, nieces and nephews; addiction does not have a preference, it does not discriminate. It is like the devil, when it feels the least bit of weakness it makes its way in and takes over the mind, body and it will quickly steal your soul. Addiction will rob the innocence from a young man, and turn the purest girl into a whore.

Drug and alcohol addiction makes people do the unthinkable. Some addicts commit horrible crimes to pay for their addiction like robbing from their families or neighbors, taking things from them they know are irreplaceable to sale or pawn just so they can get their fix for that day. They steal credit cards, cash, and even someone's identity. They abandon their children, the same children they loved, cherished and prayed over before their addiction, the same children that they would not let cross the street or watch scary movies on TV. They abandoned their children without thinking how they must feel and what their children's lives had turned into, the insecurities they now have, the sadness their hearts hold and the sleepless nights they endured while wondering where their parents are and if they are going to wake up to them or not see them for weeks or months. These children have been forgotten about like they never existed, they are left behind so their parents could use freely and not have to worry about them. They do not see their children's tears or hear their cries because they are not there. Addicts will lose their jobs because they cannot focus on them anymore; they also have found other ways to make money from the streets so "real" work does not play a role in their life. They may have binges where they cannot function in the work force causing them to get fired or not show up. They will lie to hide their addiction, make up stories so detailed we believe them. Lie about why they look like they do, why they do not have their kids, or where their money goes. Lie to our faces about their lives and manipulate us to help with their addiction. Getting us to do things for them like give them money, they make us feel sorry for them so we put our lives on hold to accommodate them and get nothing in return. We let them borrow things in promise we will get it back. They will promise us things like they will turn their lives around, get the help they need in order for us to do things for them. Their promises go unfulfilled. They cheat on their spouses because their addiction has left them with no morals, no respect for themselves or anyone else. They have a desire to feel wanted, but look for it in the wrong places. Addiction will cause them to quickly lose their every sense of direction. They lose their homes, the foundation of where they once had their stability, their securities, family pictures, memories, and dignity. They now "couch surf" jumping from one house to the next in hopes to regain that "home" feeling again. Some turn to prostitution; trading sex for drugs and alcohol. The most sacred and valued part of their body that they were taught to respect they now use to support their addiction, letting strangers take advantage of them, putting themselves at risk for sexual transmitted diseases, hepatitis and AIDS. They allow others to abuse them sexually, verbally and mentally, sacrificing their bodies to torment, just so they can feed their addiction. Some addicts will overdose and die. Some will die due to what their addiction has done to their bodies; they can only handle so much. They ultimately shut down and fail resulting in having a heart attack, organ failure, and or seizures. Sadly some addicts will take their own lives, feeling they are worthless and there is no turning it around. They're in the darkest moment in their life; they feel alone, scared, hopeless, ashamed, and feel they cannot help themselves.

"Our life is but a dream

Full of fairy tales we drown in a stream

We love, laugh and cry

In the end we will all die

The memories we create

Lie deep within our fate

The stories we tell

Could send us to Hell

We put God in our hearts

So the devil cannot shred us apart

Soon we will all live happily ever after

In Heaven full of smiles and laughter."

When I was raised, addiction, drugs and alcohol were not a part of our life. We lived a "normal" childhood and had "normal" parents. We had curfews, rules, my parents were always home in the evenings and on the weekends. We loved, laughed, cried, got in trouble; we celebrated life to the fullest. My parents taught us as much as they knew.

My dad was a hard worker and devoted his life to his family. He attended school functions, our sports games, band concerts, and drill team shows. Alcohol was not a part of him, we really did not know much about it when we were younger or see it in our home. As I got older my parents taught us how to be responsible and how to not use drugs or drink alcohol if we were to go out. I had never seen my dad drunk growing up, it was weird if I even saw him drink a beer at a restaurant. He was devoted to his family and his career. He was a genuine man who loved being a husband, father and a pappy. He was our families "rock". He held us together and everyone respected and loved him. If anyone ever needed anything they knew they could call him and he would always be willing to help. He was strict when he had to be, sincere when needed and he had a kind heart.

My dad learned the hard way when his life took an unexpected turn. His business started going downhill shortly after 9/11. He was a self-employed landscaper and work was hard to find. He did amazing work and was highly educated in this field. He studied horticultural in school, had an artistic eye and could create the most amazing designs. After a while of not finding good work and not being able to pay the bills, stress and depression set in. When he would find jobs he would not have the funds to finish them because his overhead was too high. These jobs would go unfinished for quite some time. This was devastating to him. He took pride in the quality of his work and when he could not please his customers this left him heartbroken. Soon the phone calls and threats started. Unhappy customers would call and leave the most grotesque voice mails for him to hear. Telling him he was a disgrace to mankind, scum of the earth, a mistake at birth, the most awful things you could think of, they would say. They would cuss him out, criticize his manhood and repeatedly talk down on him. Many threatened him with lawsuits, told him they would take everything he had in his possession, his home, his reputation, and his family. Some threatened to humiliate and slander him on the news for not being able to complete the work in a timely manner. He would openly talk to the clients and explain his struggles and that he was trying, but they were all so selfish they looked at him like he was a no body. They tormented him to no end and it weighed heavily on his heart. I listened to these voicemails with a hole in my heart and a lump in my throat. How could these people be so heartless and say these things to another human? He helplessly allowed them to break his pride and destroy his self-worth. Their harsh words left him feeling hopeless and he started to believe the things they would say to him. We tried to lift his spirits and tell him not to worry, that everything would be alright and work out, but it is hard to turn someone's pride around when it was so shot down. My dad was such a people pleaser and a man who loved to take care of people that when he realized he could no longer please his clients or felt he could not adequately take care of his family that is when his addiction took the best of him. Without the proper coping skills for stress and depression or the resources to get help with the finances he was lost. He was raised to be a man that provided for his family and not to reach out when times get tough. The only thing he knew he could turn to that would help ease his pain and stress was alcohol. When addiction took over his life you could imagine how shocked we all were. Not this man, this is not who he was. But this experience has taught me that it is true, addiction can happen to anyone.

<u>Reality of addiction</u>

"The addict in your life most likely started using as a quick and easy way out of their own reality and before they knew it, it became the reality of all they know."

Addiction doesn't happen the moment someone picks up a drink or experiments with drugs.

Here are some popular known drugs and their average progression rates:

Alcohol is average of 10 to 30 years.

Benzodiazepines (Xanax, Valium, and Klonipin) average 5 to 10 years.

Cocaine is average 2 to 10 years.

Crack is average 1 to 5 years.

Marijuana is average 10 to 30 years.

Crystal Meth is average 2 to 7 years.

Opiates (Heroin, OxyContin, and Vicodin) is average 2 to 7 years. (Lee, 2007 p. 13).

Of course, not everyone is the same and their addictive personalities are different.

It does not matter what an addict looks like, the color of their skin, how many teeth they have, if they have showered recently, if their voice is raspy or deep, if they are educated or not, if they twitch or have shaky hands, how many tattoos they may have or the scars and sores on their skin. They are just like you and me, unlike us though they have been to the gates of hell. They thirst for love and nourishment just like us. They crave healing, but do not know how to accept it. They feel ashamed of themselves and embarrassed. Most addicts feel they are at the lowest point in their life (even if they have not hit rock bottom yet) and they just cannot see through to the other side to realize that it does not have to be this way. They feel they have caused too much damage already and do not know where to begin to start their life over. They don't want people to know how bad they really are because then they are scared of losing any pride or self-dignity that they may have left. Some are in so deep with their drug or alcohol that it has overpowered their mind and body to where they can't even think for themselves anymore, their substance does it for them. So in the end they just simply give up and let the addiction win, resulting in losing their lives.

We do not know everything an addict has been through in their life that has caused them to become an addict in the first place. That small smile or nice gesture may just be what they need to feel love for that day; it may even give them a little hope. So instead of staring at an addict or treating them like a piece of trash, try a different approach, you may even save their life for that day. That addict you saw walking down the street may have wanted to commit suicide today thinking there was no hope left for them. The smile you gave them or the simple "hello" as you passed by may have just given them the hope they needed for that day to make them realize they are important and are still recognized and loved in society.

These addicts you see are someone's sons and daughters, moms and dads, cousins, aunts, uncles and friends. They are all children of God just like you and me.

I remember something my dad said to me one night after a binge. He said that "sometimes life just isn't worth living." The moment you hear that coming from the one person who is supposed to give you hope for the future you lose all control of your own emotions and you want to do everything in your power to save this person, (that is how I felt) but in reality you cannot. That is the hardest thing I had to learn and the main thing that has helped me recover. Knowing that no matter what you do, no matter how hard you pray and ask God to give this addict the strength to want to better themselves, no matter how many times you have poured your heart and soul out to this person, or even conducted an intervention, or trying to research all the resources they may need to help themselves. It is up to the addicts own personal perseverance to turn it all around. The guilt knowing that everything you have done has not worked will eat you up inside, but you will have to come to the realization that you have done all you can do. I am not saying to give up on your addict, but there comes a time when for your own sanity that you have to sit back and let life take its course. This life truly is in God's hands.

If the addict truly wants to change then they will take the steps to do it. When the addict does make the choice to change no matter how mad or upset you are with them they will need your love and support 100% to help them start their life changing choice.

"In the beginning you made the choice to use, quickly you became addicted and now you feel helpless, lost, confused and defeated. You feel as though you might have a disease and you cannot stop.......but in reality you have a choice. "

<u>Irony of addiction</u>

"I do not believe anyone wakes up and says to themselves, today is the day I want to be an addict. I believe they are blindsided by their own addiction as well as the loved ones around them."

I remember another heart breaking thing my dad said to me one night. I was at his house trying once again to talk to him and understand what he was going through and trying to figure out any ways I could help him. He said to me with pain in his eyes "I drink because I don't feel good, but I don't feel good because I drink". He was sick with the alcohol and he was sick without the alcohol. He was drinking to suppress his pain because mentally he did not feel good, but drinking also made him sick and not feel good, but at this point he had to drink because without the alcohol in his body he could not function. It took me a while to understand what he meant, but once I understood the seriousness in his body's chemical addiction it was like a knife ripped my heart. To me it seemed he did not even enjoy drinking, (like we thought) but had to because not only was his mind addicted his body was chemically addicted as well.

I was also told a few years later by a meth addict that smoking meth doesn't even get him high anymore, but yet he still did it because his body needed it and he felt he had nothing left to lose.

Do you see the irony in this? Most of the time we think the addicts enjoy the drug or alcohol they are using, but in reality after a while they hate it and often feel ashamed of themselves after they have consumed or used. They find themselves unable to do normal everyday tasks without the drug/alcohol. Even though they may not want to use that day, they have to in order to feel somewhat normal. That is the irony with addiction. The way the drug/alcohol takes over is not something they choose. Even though they willingly chose to use in the beginning, and they can still choose to get better, the drug/alcohol quickly turns into their food, their water, their nourishment and their only means of survival.

Addiction takes lives

I did a small survey and asked people if they were given a choice on how they would like to pass away what it would be. I gave them the choice of natural causes, cancer and addiction.

Not one person chose addiction to be their cause of death, but so many people die from this sickness every day because they refused get help.

A lot of celebrities, musicians and famous people we see in the public battle addiction. Most people think because they have tons of money and can afford fancy rehabs and treatment centers they will be saved from their addiction. This is untrue. The addict has to truly want it.

To prove that money and fame cannot save a person from their addiction and neither can fancy rehabs or treatment centers. Here is a long but relatively short list of actors/actresses, musicians and athletes that were defeated by their addiction.

1. Herb Adams-Professional wrestling promoter, heart complications due to drug abuse.
2. Nick Adams- Actor, drug overdose.
3. David Allen Adkisson- Professional wrestler, death speculated by drug overdose.
4. Ryunosuke Akutagawa- Writer, overdose on barbiturates.
5. Dennis Allen- Infamous drug dealer, heart failure due to drugs.

6. GG Allin- Punk musician, heroin overdose.
7. Bridgette Anderson- Former child actress, alcohol and heroin overdose.
8. Matthew Ansara- Actor and body builder, heroin overdose.
9. Chris Antly- Champion horse race jockey, drug related causes.
10. West Arkeen- Musician, drug overdose.
11. Howard Arkley- Painter, drug overdose.
12. Kevyn Aucoin- Photographer and makeup artist, kidney and liver failure, prescription painkiller addiction.
13. Florence Ballard- Musician, The Supremes, cardiac arrest due to long term drug abuse.
14. Lester Bangs- Musician, writer, overdose on painkillers.
15. Jean-Michael Baquiat- Painter, heroin overdose.
16. Scotty Beckett- Former child actor, barbiturate overdose.
17. Bix Beiderbecke- Jazz musician, alcoholism.
18. Steve Bechler- Major League baseball pitcher, died from using ephedrine.
19. John Belushi- Blues Brothers, actor and comedian, heroin and cocaine overdose.
20. Bunny Berigan- Musician, cirrhosis of the liver due to alcoholism.
21. George Best- Ex football player, Manchester United, multiple organ failure from long term alcoholism.
22. Len Bias- Basketball star, cocaine overdose.
23. Bam Bam Bigelow- Professional wrestler, cocaine and temazepam overdose.
24. Count Gottfried Von Bismark- Aristocrat, drug overdose.
25. Matty Blagg (Mathew Roberts) Musician, heart attack due to ketamine and ecstasy overdose.
26. Mike Bloomfield- Blues guitarist, heroin overdose.
27. Tommy Bolin- Musician, Deep Purple, drugs and alcohol poisoning.
28. Jon Bonham- Musician Led Zepplin, alcohol related asphyxiation caused by choking on his own vomit.
29. James Booker- Musician, liver failure.
30. Christopher Bowman- Professional ice skater, prescription drug overdose.
31. Elisa Bridges- Model, acute intoxication, combined

effects of heroin, methamphetamine, meperidine and alprazolam.

32. Erik Brodreskift- Musician, Borknager, Gorgoroth, and Immortal. Pill overdose.
33. Herman Brood- Musician, long term substance abuse.
34. Dennis Brown- Musician, reggae singer, cardiac arrest and collapsed lung related to chronic drug abuse.
35. Lenny Bruce- Comedian, morphine overdose.
36. Rob Buck- Musician, 10,000 Maniacs, liver disease.
37. Tim Buckley- Rock and roll musician, heroin overdose.
38. Chad Butler aka Pimp C- Rap musician, accidental overdose, promethazine/codeine mixed with his medical condition, sleep apnea.
39. Paul Butterfield- Musician, drug related heart failure.
40. Andres Caicedo- Writer, drug overdose, 60 pills of secobarbital in his system.
41. Casey Calvert- Guitarist of Hawthorne Heights, accidental drug overdose, mixture of opiates, citalopram and clonazepam.
42. Ken Caminiti- Former major league baseball player, acute cocaine and opiates intoxication.
43. Max Canter- Journalist and actor, became an addict while researching addicts in New York. Heroin overdose.
44. Truman Capote- Writer, liver disease, complication due to multiple drug intoxication.
45. Gia Carangi- Supermodel, heroin abuse led to death from AIDS.
46. Leroy Carr- Blues musician, cirrhosis of the liver as a result of alcoholism.
47. Gene Clark- Musician, bleeding ulcer due to long term alcohol abuse.
48. Sonny Clark- Musician, hard pop pianist, heroin overdose.
49. Steve Clark- Musician Def Leppard, accidental death, anti-depressants, alcohol and pain killers.
50. Michael Clark- Musician, The Byrds, liver failure due to long term alcoholism.

51. Montgomery Clift- Actor, heart attack due to severe alcoholism and drug abuse.
52. Kurt Cobain- Musician, Nirvana, heroin overdose and shotgun wound to the head.
53. Natasha Collins- Actress, cocaine overdose.
54. Brian Cole- Musician, The Associates, heroin overdose.
55. Brian Connely- Musician, liver damage caused by long term substance abuse and chronic alcoholism.
56. Megan Connolly- Actress, heroin overdose.
57. Pamela Courson- Common law wife of Jim Morrison from The Doors, heroin overdose.
58. Cowboy (Keith Wiggins) Musician, Grandmaster Flash and Furious Five, drug overdose.
59. Carl Crack- Musician, Arti Teenage Riot, drug overdose.
60. Darby Crash- Punk musician The Germs, heroin overdose.
61. Robbin Crosby- Musician, contracted HIV as a result of long term heroin addiction and heroin overdose.
62. Dalida- Singer, barbiturates overdose.
63. Dorothy Dandridge- Actress, Singer, anti-depressant overdose.
64. Eileen Davies- Alternative rock singer/songwriter, heroin overdose.
65. Jesse Ed Davis- Guitarist, session musician, drug overdose.
66. Paul Demayo- Professional bodybuilder, heroin overdose.
67. Teri Diver- pornographic actress, cardiac arrest caused by overdose of migraine medication.
68. Kiki Djan- Musician, drug addiction and AIDS.
69. DJ Screw- Musician, heart attack, codeine overdose.
70. Desmond Donnelly- Politician, businessman, journalist, alcohol and barbiturates overdose.
71. Tommy Dorsey- Jazz musician and band leader, choked to death while sleeping with the aid of sleeping pills.
72. John Dougherty- Musician, heroin overdose.
73. Eric Douglas- Standup comedian, acute intoxication by the effects of alcohol, tranquilizers, and pain killers.
74. Nick Drake- Musician, anti-depressant overdose.
75. Michael Dransfield- Poet, heroin overdose.
76. Bobby Driscoll- Actor, heart failure, long term drug

abuse.

77. Kevin Dubrow- Rock vocalist, cocaine overdose.
78. Bobby Duncan Jr- Professional wrestler, prescription drug overdose.
79. Anthony Durante- Professional wrestler, drug overdose.
80. Jeanne Eagels- Actress, alcohol and heroin abuse.
81. Tommy Edwards- Musician, brain aneurysm due to alcoholism.
82. John Entwistle- Musician, bassist for the Who, heart failure from cocaine use.
83. Brian Epstein- Manager of the Beatles, drug overdose.
84. Rick Evers- Musician, drummer and song writer, heroin overdose.
85. Chris Farley- Comedian, cocaine and morphine overdose.
86. Pete Farndon- Musician, The Pretenders, heroin overdose.
87. Rainer Werner Fassbinder- Play writer and director, cocaine overdose, possible suicide.
88. Brenda Fassie- Singer, cocaine overdose.
89. W.C Fields- Performer and actor, complications of alcohol.
90. Aaron Flahavan- Professional English football goal keeper, died drunk driving.
91. Althea Flynt- Co-publisher of Hustler magazine, drowned in her bathtub after passing out from drug overdose.
92. Zac Foley- Musician, overdose from heroin, cocaine, ecstasy, temazepam, barbiturates and alcohol.
93. Katy French- Super model and socialite, cocaine use.
94. Sigmund Freud- Neurologist, long term cocaine use, physician assisted morphine overdose.
95. Rory Gallagher- Musician, pneumonia and liver failure, side effect of combination of doctor prescribed drugs.
96. Paul Gardiner- Musician, drug overdose.
97. Lowell George- Musician, heart attack, due to drug abuse.
98. Talitha Getty- Actress and socialite, heroin overdose.
99. Andy Gibb- Singer, long term cocaine and alcohol abuse.
100. Simon Gipps Kent- Actor, morphine poisoning, suspected drug overdose.

101. Candy Givens- Musician, drowned in a Jacuzzi after passing out due to alcohol and quaaludes.
102. Trevor Goddard- Former professional boxer turned actor, cocaine, heroin, hydrocodone and diazepam overdose.
103. Paul Gonsalves- Jazz tenor saxophonist, narcotics overdose.
104. Lucy Grealy- Poet, presumed accidental drug overdose.
105. Sean Greenway- Indie musician, heroin overdose.
106. Gribouille- Singer, lethal mixture of alcohol and medications.
107. Eddie Guerro- Professional wrestler, drug use led to heart attack.
108. Stacy Guess- Musician, heroin overdose.
109. Clinton Haines- Noted computer hacker, heroin over dose 21st birthday.
110. Paul Hammond- Musician, drug overdose.
111. Bobby Hatfield- Musician, heart attack by cocaine overdose.
112. Tim Hardin- Folk musician, heroin and morphine overdose.
113. Brynn Hartman- Wife and murderer of comedian Phil Hartman, suicide after cocaine and alcohol.
114. Alex Harvey- Musician, liver damage caused by alcohol abuse.
115. Phyllis Haver- Actress, barbiturate overdose, suicide.
116. James Hayden- Actor, heroin overdose.
117. Joey Hawthorne- Professional poker player, drug overdose.
118. Eddie Hazel- Musician, liver failure and internal bleeding due to drug and alcohol use.
119. Mitch Hedberg- Comedian, cocaine and heroin overdose.
120. Helno (Noel Rota) - Musician, died trying to overcome a serious drug addiction.
121. Tim Hemensley- Indie Musician, heroin overdose.
122. Margaux Hemingway- Actress, disputed suicide, overdose of phenobarbital.
123. Jimi Hendrix- Rock and roll musician, respiratory arrest caused by alcohol and barbiturate overdose and vomit inhalation.
124. Curt Henning- Professional wrestler, cocaine overdose.

125. Gino Hernandez- Wrestler, cocaine overdose.
126. Billie Holiday- Jazz singer, cirrhosis of the liver, longtime alcohol and heroin use.
127. Hollywood Fats- Musician, heroin overdose.
128. Gary Holton- Actor, alcohol and morphine overdose.
129. James Honeyman Scott- Musician, cocaine overdose.
130. Whitney Houston- Accidental drowning, cocaine use and possible heart disease.
131. Shannon Hoon- Musician, Blind Melon, cocaine overdose.
132. Howard Hughes- Aviator, engineer, industrialist, movie producer, playboy. Liver failure, lethal amounts of codeine and valuim.
133. Phyllis Hyman- Singer, suicide involving lethal amounts of pentobarbital and secobarbital.
134. Julio Jaramillo- Singer, liver damage caused by alcohol.
135. Steven Ronald "Stevo" Jensen- Musician, The Vandals, prescription overdose.
136. Joelle- American born French singer, drug overdose.
137. Michael Jackson- Singer, propofol intoxication.
138. Anissa Jones- Actress, accidental overdose of cocaine, angel dust, Quaaludes and seconal.
139. Brian Jones- Musician, The Rolling Stones, likely alcohol and barbiturate intoxication.
140. Rob Jones (aka The Bass Thing) Musician, heroin, cocaine, and alcohol overdose.
141. Russell Jones (aka Ol' Dirty Bastard) - Hip hop musician, accidental overdose, cocaine and prescription pain killers.
142. Janis Joplin- Rock and roll and blues musician, heroin overdose.
143. John Kahn- Musician, heart disease, heroin, cocaine and antidepressants found in body.
144. David Kennedy- Fourth child of Robert Kennedy, cocaine and Demerol overdose.
145. Jack Kerouac- Writer and poet, complications due to alcohol.
146. Bernard Kettlewell- Medical doctor, drug overdose.

147. Dorothy Kilgallen- Irish-American journalist, fatal combination of alcohol and seconal.
148. Paul Kossoff- Musician, drug related heart problems.
149. Eddie Kurdziel- Musician, drug overdose.
150. Alan Ladd- Actor, acute overdose of alcohol and barbiturates.
151. Arcadia Lake- Pornographic actress, drug overdose.
152. Barbara La Marr- Actress, drug related.
153. Karen Lancaume- Pornographic actress, overdose of temazepam.
154. Carole Landis- Actress, overdose of barbiturates.
155. Heath Ledger- Actor, accidental death combined drug intoxication of various prescription drugs, oxycodone, hydrocodone, temazepam and others.
156. Frank X. Leyendecker- Illustrator, drug overdose.
157. Debbie Linden- Glamour model and actress, heroin overdose.
158. Ruan Lingyu- Silent film actress, overdose of barbiturates.
159. Eugene Lipscomb- American football player, heroin overdose.
160. Mike Lockwood- Professional wrestler, choked on his vomit after overdose of painkillers and alcohol.
161. Trinity Loren- Porn star, model and stripper, overdose of prescription painkillers.
162. Bela Lugosi- Actor, drug related overdose.
163. Zoe Tamerlis Lund- Former child musician prodigy turned model, actress, and writer, heart failure due to heroin use.
164. Donyale Luna- Musician, heroin overdose.
165. Aaron Lynch- Writer, opiate-based painkiller overdose.
166. Phil Lynott- Musician, heart failure caused by alcohol and drug use.
167. Billy Mackenzie- Musician, overdose of temazepam. amitriptyline and paracetamol.
168. Bibek Maitra- Politician, drug overdose.
169. Sherri Martel- Professional wrestler, overdose, multiple drugs, including high amounts of oxycodone.
170. Billy Martin- Major League baseball player and manager, alcohol-related auto accident.

171. James McCallum Bronson- Stepson of actor Charles Bronson, drug overdose.
172. Ron "Pigpen" McKernan- Musician, The Grateful Dead, gastrointestinal hemorrhage linked to alcohol abuse.
173. Robbie McIntosh- Musician, heroin overdose.
174. Jonathan Melvoin- Touring keyboardist for Smashing Pumpkins, heroin overdose.
175. Big Maceo Merriweather- Blues pianist, chronic alcoholism.
176. Mighty Spoiler- Calypso music singer, alcohol-related illness.
177. Miss Christine- Musician, heroin overdose.
178. Marilyn Monroe- Actress, overdose of barbiturate-based sleeping pills.
179. Keith Moon- Musician, The Who, overdose on antiseizure medication prescribed for alcoholism.
180. Chester Morris- Actor, drug overdose.
181. Billy Murcia- Musician, accidental suffocation after drug and alcohol use.
182. Brent Mydland- Musician, keyboardist of The Grateful Dead, cocaine and morphine overdose.
183. My Dad- Business owner, dad, pappy, friend, husband, all around American guy- Heart attack due to acute alcohol intoxication.
184. Modest Mussorgsky- Classical composer, alcohol related.
185. Delpine Neid- Musician, The Nuns, drug overdose.
186. Joachim Nielsn- Musician, drug overdose.
187. Bradley Nowell- Musician, Sublime, heroin overdose.
188. Hugh O'Connor- Actor, suicide under influence of cocaine.
189. Lani O'Grady- Actress, multiple drug intoxication.
190. Johnny O'Keefe- Musician and singer, heart attack due to prescription drug addiction.
191. Christina Onassis- Daughter of billionaire Aristotle Onassis, pulmonary edema, caused by drug abuse and dramatic weight changes.
192. Bryan Ottoson- Musician, prescription drug overdose.

193. Malcome Owen- Singer, heroin overdose.
194. John Panozzo- Musician drummer, complications from alcohol abuse.
195. Marco Pantani- Cyclist, acute cocaine intoxication.
196. Charlie Parker- Jazz musician, pneumonia and bleeding ulcers, due to drug and alcohol abuse.
197. Robert Pastorelli- Actor, heroin overdose.
198. Gram Parsons- Country musician, overdose on morphine and tequila.
199. John Pulcine- Painter, drug overdose.
200. Kristin Pfaff- Musician, heroin overdose.
201. Esther Phillips- Musician and singer, liver and kidney failure due to alcohol and heroin abuse.
202. John Phillips- Musician, heart failure due to a lifetime of alcohol and narcotics.
203. River Phoenix- Actor, overdose on heroin and cocaine.
204. Rob Pilates- Musician, Milli Vanilli, drug overdose.
205. Dana Plato- Actress, overdose on muscle relaxers and vicodine.
206. Pola- Model in Vogue and Cosmopolitan, heroin overdose.
207. Darrell Porter- Professional baseball catcher, cocaine overdose.
208. Elvis Presley- Singer, heart attack due to overdose of barbiturates.
209. Freddie Prinze- Comic and actor, self-inflicted gunshot wound while under influence of Quaaludes.
210. Robert Quine- Musician, heroin overdose.
211. Glenn Quinn- Actor, heroin overdose.
212. Carl Radle- Bass guitarist, kidney disease from long term alcohol and narcotics use.
213. Dee Dee Ramone- Musician, heroin overdose.
214. James Ray- Singer, drug overdose.
215. Johnnie Ray- Musician, liver failure caused by alcoholism.
216. Michael Reeves- Film Director, barbiturate overdose.
217. Jimmy Reilly- Musician, heroin overdose.
218. Elis Regina- Singer, fatal alcohol and temazepam interaction.
219. Brad Renfro- Actor, heroin and morphine overdose.

220. Rachel Roberts- Actor, barbiturate overdose.
221. Andy Rogers- Musician, heroin overdose.
222. Michael Rudetsky- Musician, heroin overdose.
223. David Ruffin- Musician, drug overdose.
224. George Sanders- Actor, barbiturates overdose.
225. Catya Sassoon- Model, actress, overdose on hydro morphine and cocaine.
226. Joe Schermie- Musician, heart attack from long term drug abuse.
227. Bon Scott- Musician- AC/DC, acute alcohol poisoning.
228. Ronnie Scott- Jazz tenor saxophonist and jazz club owner, died from mixture of alcohol and temazepam.
229. Jean Seberg- Actress, barbiturate and alcohol overdose.
230. Rod Scurry- Major League baseball pitcher, cocaine induced heart attack.
231. Nerine Shatner- Wife of actor William Shatner, drowned in pool while intoxicated. Traces of diazepam in blood stream.
232. Will Shatter- Musician, heroin overdose.
233. Bobby Sheehan- Musician, drug overdose.
234. Eric Show- Baseball player, cocaine and heroin overdose.
235. Judee Sill- folk Musician, heroin overdose.
236. Don Simpson- Film producer, heart attack, over 20 drugs in his system at time of death.
237. Hillel Slovak- Musician, Red Hot Chili Peppers, heroin overdose.
238. Anna Nicole Smith- Playboy playmate and actress, lethal combination of chloral hydrate and various benzodiazepines.
239. Robert Smith- Saxophonist, heart attack due to life time of alcohol abuse.
240. Freddy Soto- Comedian, writer and actor, lethal mixture of alcohol, alprazolam and fentanyl.
241. Layne Staley- Musician, Alice and Chains, cocaine and heroin overdose.
242. Joey Stefano- Pornographic actor, overdose of cocaine, morphine, heroin and ketamine.

243. Rory Storm- Musician, overdose of sleeping pills.
244. Maragaret Sullavan- Actress, barbiturate overdose.
245. Paige Summers- Actress, overdose from painkillers, codeine and oxycodone.
246. Vinnie Taylor- Musician, heroin overdose.
247. Gary Thain- Musician, drug overdose.
248. Jason Thirsk- Musician, Pennywise, suicide from depression and alcohol treatment.
249. Johnny Thunders- Musician, The New York Dolls, alcohol and methadone poisoning.
250. Dylan Thomas- Poet, chronic alcoholism.
251. John Thompson- Poet, lethal mixture of barbiturates and alcohol.
252. Ike Turner- Musician, producer, cocaine overdose with high blood pressure and emphysema with contributing factors.
253. Paul Vaessen- Former professional football player, drug overdose.
254. Paul Van- Magazine editor, drug overdose.
255. Sid Vicious- Musician- Sex Pistols, heroin overdose.
256. Gene Vincent- Rock and roll musician, liver damage caused by alcohol.
257. Robert Hudson Walker- Actor, died suddenly after being administered sodium amytal by his doctor.
258. Dinah Washington- Musician, singer, overdose on diet pills and alcohol.
259. Dave Waymer- American football defensive back, cocaine induced heart attack.
260. Michael Weber- Lead guitarist of the Seminal Rats, heroin overdose.
261. Brett Whiteley- Artist, heroin and temazepam overdose.
262. Amy Whinehouse- British singer, alcohol poisoning.
263. Kurt Winter- Guitarist with The Guess Who, kidney failure from sustained drug abuse.
264. Keith Whitley- Country musician, alcohol poisoning.
265. Dale Whittington- Race car driver, drug overdose.
266. Alan Wilson- Musician, The Canned Meat, drug overdose.
267. Dennis Wilson- Musician, The Beach Boys, alcohol related drowning.

268. Kenneth Williams- Actor, author and comedian, overdose of barbiturates.
269. Linda Wong- Pornographic actress, overdose on alprazolam, chloral hydrate and alcohol.
270. Natalie Wood- Actress, drowned when intoxicated.

Did you notice #183? My Dad. I added him to the list because even though he did not have fame or fortunes like the others they all have something in common. They were all defeated by their addiction. They all left their mark in this world, whether they were famously publicized or a normal everyday person. They all experienced the repercussions of what addiction does.

Ketamine- Is a potent analgesic that is usually used in brief or small surgical procedures. It can create hallucinations, confusion and disorientation.

Alprazolam- Is prescribed for anxiety.

Fentanyl- Is a potent narcotic, commonly used with a sedative and anti-psychotic drug to help with anesthesia.

Benzodiazepines- Is commonly prescribed for anxiety and insomnia, but can be used as a tranquilizer.

Chloral Hydrate- Is prescribed for anxiety, insomnia, and tension.

Heroin- Is a morphine like drug that has no use in the medical field.

Steroids- Is a substance that contains a large amount of hormones.

Morphine- Is a white crystalline alkaloid often administered for severe pain.

Cocaine- Is a white crystalline powder. Causes a euphoric feeling. Has no use in the medical field.

Barbiturate- Is prescribed for seizures.

Codeine- Is used to treat mild or moderate pain, diarrhea, and cough.

Methadone- Is prescribed for the relief of severe pain. Addicts going through detox with severe pain may be treated with methadone.

Diazepam- Is prescribed for anxiety, nervous tension, muscle spasm, and is used as an anticonvulsant.

Temazepam- Is prescribed for Insomnia.

Secobarbital- Is prescribed for insomnia, agitation, and as an anticonvulsant and preoperative sedative.

Sodium Amytal- Is trademark for a Barbiturate.

Propofol- This is intravenously administered by a doctor. It is a general anesthesia.

Tranquilizers- Is prescribed to calm anxious or agitated people.

Hydromorphone- Is prescribed to treat moderate to severe pain.

Ecstasy- Is a drug that induces a euphoric state. No use in the medical field.

Methamphetamine- Is prescribed to treat narcolepsy and hyperkinesia and helps reduce the appetite in obese people.

Meperidine- Is used to treat severe pain or anxiety usually before surgery.

Promethazine- Is prescribed motion sickness, nausea, and rhinitis.

Oxycodone- Is prescribed to treat moderate or severe pain.

Quaaludes- Is a trademark for a sedative-hypnotic. This drug is no longer distributed in the United States.

Angel Dust- Is a white crystalline powder. Chemical known as PCP. Causes euphoria, loss of inhibitions, anxiety, disorientation, restlessness, drowsiness, disorganized thinking. Has no use in the medical field.

Seconal- Is a trademark for a sedative-hypnotic.

Demoral- Is prescribed to relieve moderate to severe pain. Similar to morphine.

Amitriptyline- Is prescribed to treat depression.

Paracetamol- Is a nonprescription pain reliever. Acetaminophen.

Pentobarbital- Is prescribed to treat seizures and for sedation

(Coon, *et al* , 1998, pp.

898,64,625,183,320,756,1541,1051,358,1022,484,1593,1465

,81,1637,784,1022,1013,1331,1179,1368,1465,75,1231).

Did you notice that most of these drugs are prescribed for anxiety, depression, agitation, nervous tension and pain? Most all of these issues are underlining problems that occur with people that are addicts.

Nearly 90% of all suicide victims experience issues with substance abuse and or depression leading up to their deaths.

Is addiction a genetic disease?

"My greatest fear is that my kids and your kids will become addicts if we do not openly talk with them about life and addiction."

Many people will debate back and forth. Scientist and doctors will always have their tests and studies to prove or disprove if addiction is a genetic disease, mental disease or a moral choice. While the studies are still being done, we are still and always will be left with the crude aspects of addiction.

There are many families that have histories of addiction. I do not believe we will ever know if addiction is linked genetically or if it is the upbringing that we raise our children in that creates the addict. We all know addiction affects everyone in the family. Could these negative effects that addictions have on the families and the lack of education, acceptance of one another, and the ability to cope with an addictive family member be what create more addicts? Could the addictive parent not offering hope for their children or being open about their addiction leave their children in the dark with no other outlook on life but addiction? Or the addict that has the excuse in their mind that a family member was an addict, therefore their actions can be excused because it is a "family disease?"

If you look at the cycle of family addiction, it seems that the cycle cannot be broken. My conclusion on this is because there will always be the excuse that this is a family disease, because someone in the family was an addict. With that excuse and always having a reason to fall back on, why would anyone feel the need to change? It is a way of self-enabling. Often you hear of parents being addicts or uncles, aunts or cousins. I wonder if anyone ever sat down with the families of these addicts and explained in detail what addiction is and how to cope without turning to drugs and alcohol themselves? Somehow, the cycle has to be broken with addiction. Many of us are taught the basics in life, but are we taught how to practice healthy living habits and how not to become an addict? Yes, in the end it is up to the person to decide if they will use or not.

Though we will never fully understand or really have all the answers to these questions, what we do know is that once addiction sets in, it sickens the mind and body. How we learn to cope with it will affect our future and the future of addicts.

Growing up, both of my parents were addicts. I never experienced their love or affection that I so badly craved from them. I lived in foster care as a child. When I was eleven, I got to live with my dad. I never had a relationship with my mother due to her addiction. I wanted to be accepted and liked more than anything in the world (especially from my parents). I needed unconditional love and I was not getting it. When I was twelve, I was taking Old Style to school in my Wonder Woman thermos. I moved out when I was sixteen. When I turned 21 my alcoholism was in full swing. I was addicted to anything that would help me escape from uncomfortable situations and dull my feelings from my reality. Growing up I was never taught to deal with life any different. My drugs of choice were alcohol, Xanax, Heroin and Morphine. I was a "functioning" addict; I worked at the Bureau of Motor Vehicles. When I was 25, I got married and had two children a year apart. When I was 30, I went to treatment. I did not do it for myself; I did it for my kids and husband. I completed the program and stayed clean for only 90 days. I have a spinal condition that results in me taking pain killers. That soon became my drug of choice. I began to "doctor shop" I was getting prescriptions for opiates, benzos, morphine patches and fentynol. When the prescriptions ran out and I could not get any more I got into smack, otherwise known as heroin. This was cheaper and easier to find. At this point in my life I was living in my basement. For two years I hid down there away from the world and my family. I woke up every day and had to "fix" myself so I would not get violently sick. I stayed high and drunk 24/7. I wanted to die, but I wouldn't. No matter how many drugs I took or how much alcohol I drank it would not kill me. My kids would come down to bring me food, but I would be so high I would not be able to eat.

In September of 2009 I had had enough. I found out that Nikki Sixx of the Motley Crue was in recovery and if he could do it, so could I. And besides I would not die so I figured I must have been put on this earth do be or do something. I had no idea though, what my future had in store for me.

I made the choice to go to a treatment center in Plymouth Indiana. I completed an intensive outpatient treatment for six weeks and I am currently attending AA meetings. I had no other choice but to listen to the other women in the program. They knew how to stay sober. The women not only helped me stay sober, they taught me how to be a better mother, a better daughter and a better friend. They taught me what it was like to love, live and enjoy life. I was never taught any of this before. I still learn on a daily basis how to stay clean and sober one day at a time.

My husband and I divorced after 15 years of marriage. I realized he was one of the biggest enablers in my life. I was drunk and high throughout our entire marriage and as soon as I came to know him sober, I did not like him. When I was living at home I felt like a square peg trying to live in a round hole. No one understood me or could relate to my feelings. I realized when sober, I could live a happy life outside of the basement I once hid in. I gained independence and it felt good. My ex-husband and I share custody of our two children. My son felt bitterness towards me the first few months out of the divorce. Both my kids attended Ala-teen to learn about addiction and how to handle their own feelings and how to cope with life's ups and downs. They now understand me and how I have changed to live a happier healthier life. Our relationships are so much better now and I can offer them the love I never had growing up.

I found happiness at AA meetings and felt comfortable around people that were like me. That is where I finally felt "at home." I had never had a real "home" before as a child. I met a man who understood me and loves me for who I am. I have never felt so comfortable in my own skin and I am truly happy.

I believe religion is for people afraid of going to hell; spirituality is for people who have already been there. When I finally believed in what I was praying for, God heard me. He helped me; He is, was and will always be there for me. I just had to find Him.

Vicki A.
A grateful recovering alcoholic/addict

Raising non-addict children

"Our childhood memories help create who we are, but the choices we make help create how we live"

It's hard to know where to begin in giving advice on how to help children cope with life's struggles, to make adjustments and changes in one's life. Children do need guidance and direction to learn how to handle the big and little bumps along the road of life. Until they are 25 years old, their prefrontal cortex is not fully developed and therefore, many mistakes and poor decisions will be made. As the adults, we sometimes must save them from themselves. They can't do "life" by themselves. One important behavior to teach children is to ask for help. So many times, I have seen children get deeper and deeper into problems, when asking for help early in their process would have alleviated some of the heartache and pain.

I also believe that we must teach children that life's struggles and problems do not define who they are. Learning to put things into perspective is essential to one's peace and serenity. Teaching children to believe in themselves, forgive themselves and love themselves is one of the most important things we can do for our children.

Peers and peer pressure seem to be other important factors that can lead a child down the wrong path. Teaching children about the importance of picking friends and leaving behind friends that are not in their best interest is oftentimes critical in a child's journey to wholeness.

Raising healthy, whole children can be the hardest job in the world and also the most rewarding one. We are all imperfect human beings and when we strive to make things perfect, we set ourselves up for hurt and disappointment. When we try to control what we can't, we drive ourselves down the road to insanity. Control and perfectionism seem to be two driving forces that give birth to addictions and compulsivity. Teaching our children how to embrace our imperfection and let go of what we can't control creates a more balanced and healthy lifestyle.

Children are vulnerable and so resilient at the same time. Vulnerable, in that, they have not developed the filters to discern what is real about whom they are and what is not. Because the people around our children are humans and make mistakes and our childlike brain believes and trusts those who are close to us, children believe even the negative things they hear about themselves. Our childhood filters or boundaries are very thin and have not developed and won't until we understand how our environment shapes us. As parents, we all want to protect our children, protect them from the struggles that we went through, hoping that they will learn from our wisdom, hoping that our protection will shield them. However, we need to balance this protectiveness, as we do with other areas of our life. When we overprotect our children and we don't allow them to make mistakes and learn how to cope with the challenges and struggles of life, we inadvertently create a theme within the child and a belief that they cannot handle their own problems. This in turn creates disappointment and pain. It creates a vacuum and so they begin to find ways to feel better about life and themselves. They find ways to take that pain, that struggle away. We do a disservice to our children when we don't teach children how to cope with the struggles of life when life gives us bumps in the road. Simply, that means allowing our children to feel the pain of disappointment, to feel the pain of changes, and teach them how to move forward in life. However, before we can do that with our children, we must be able to do that with ourselves. And when we help them cope with the pain and hurt, we are teaching them not to self-medicate but to self sooth, to self-nurture, to take care of themselves. In our society, vulnerability is sometimes looked at as a weakness. However, I find that vulnerability takes more courage than holding onto the pain. Keeping secret about our struggles creates more pain and disappointment and feels as if you're a hostage in your own body. It is in letting go of the fear of being vulnerable that allows us to see who we really are, to see that we need to embrace and accept ourselves for the humanness that we all experience. We learn to love ourselves unconditionally, to self sooth, to nurture, value and respect ourselves in a way that is healthy and not self-destructive. And so we ask ourselves, how is it that we do this? How is it that we don't do this? Society, our upbringing and childhood experiences all play a big part in why we don't do this. When we don't take care of our spiritual, emotional, physical and mental selves, we are setting ourselves up to be in pain, feel bad, to not like ourselves and therefore we turn to something; alcohol, drugs, sex, gambling or anything that will make us feel better and be able to forget the inner turmoil that we are experiencing, to escape from reality, to alter our mood. We can learn to love the "inner child" and give it what it needs, give it what it didn't get growing up, allow it to be that precious and lovable true self that has been covered up for many years. We do this so that we can heal that part of ourselves, which I believe can be the root of compulsivity and addictions.

I once did a workshop titled "R.E.V.E.A.L. the child within" and shared my thoughts and beliefs about healing the inner child and included ways of doing the healing. REVEAL..........R is for remembering the precious child within, protecting the child; E is for empathy for ourselves just as we would have for any child; V is for validation of the child which is an important step in the healing and grief process; E is for expression of all emotions, needs and wants; A is for affirmation of our uniqueness, purpose in life and believing in those affirmations; L is for love which is to nurture, spend time with, love and accept ourselves unconditionally and trust in our own inner guidance. With this process of REVEALing our inner child we can begin to heal and grieve that part of us so that we do not succumb to addictions to alter our mood or escape. When we are capable of doing these things for ourselves, we are then role models for our children. And if that child does not have *the best role model or somewhere along the way finds themselves in an addictive lifestyle, they will know that it is always possible to break free of the self-medication and begin to heal and find peace and serenity through a healthy process. It takes courage and strength to heal what is within us that has been unnoticed and unloved for so long.*

-Pamela Geisinger Sandy

MS, LPC-S

Licensed Professional Counselor

2

<u>Stages of Addiction</u>

Tolerance

After prolonged use your body becomes increasingly resistant and tolerant to your drug or other substance. Tolerance is key to what builds up the addiction.

When many start out with their drug or alcohol of choice, their tolerance is low; after prolonged use it takes longer and more to reach their level of intoxication. Starting out my dad drank martinis and scotch. After a while the effects took longer, so he started taking shots. When he was at his worst he was guzzling a 5th of vodka multiple times a day. Each bottle of vodka he consumed was equivalent to 17 shots.

Withdrawal

Withdrawal is the negative reaction the body and mind goes through when going without its drug or substance it is addicted to. The withdrawal symptoms can be life threatening and can cause physiological damage. When the addict is mentally and chemically dependent on a drug or alcohol the withdrawal stage can be very severe and may need to be done in the care of a doctor.

Withdraw is basically the beginning stages of addiction. The addict does not want to withdrawal from the drug or alcohol they are on. They continue to use to not feel those feelings and experience the discomfort and devastation the withdrawal has on the body and mind.

I wish I would have known what the withdrawal symptoms were back then. The first time I remember seeing my dad have withdrawal symptoms we thought at that time he was acting. I know differently now.

We were at my sister's house; my mom, sister, dad and myself. I don't remember exactly why we were all there; it may have been a birthday or something.

It was mid-evening and we were all in the living room hanging out having small talk and watching the kids play. I remember looking over at my dad at the time and his face was very flush, he kept fidgeting with his arms and hands like he was nervous. He did come to the house that evening a little intoxicated but not to the point where he was belligerent. As time passed I noticed he was becoming more agitated, and I could tell my mom could sense his change in mood as well. I observed him as he slowly removed himself vocally out of the conversations and focused solely on trying to control his hand movements. We all kind of left the living room at that time except for my dad; we really didn't know what was going on with him, but we could feel the tension and did not like it. We didn't talk about it when we left the room, but we all knew we were feeling the same effects. A little after we left the room I got concerned so I peeked around the corner and noticed my dad's hands shaking uncontrollably, his legs were jumping out from under him and it seemed like he wanted to get up off the couch, but he couldn't regain his balance. He was making groaning noises under his breath and he was very sweaty. I didn't know how to react to this. I played it off and told everyone it was late and time we all went home. I think my dad was relieved that I spoke up about leaving because he quickly turned his focus on me and smiled. I walked my parents out to the car and told them goodbye. What I now know that I did not know then is that he was having withdrawal symptoms from not drinking in this period he was at my sister's house. Even if I had known then what was going on I do not believe there would have been anything I could have done. At this point he was deep into the denial stage.

After that incident I started to notice this behavior more often. I also noticed when the symptoms started he would leave or seclude himself from others around him. I remember Thanksgiving one year, his hands were shaking so badly at the table he could not get his fork of food from his plate into his mouth. Every time he would get ready to try again he would look around to see if anyone was watching. Of course I was, but I don't believe anyone else was, they were engaged in their own food and conversations. He tried numerous times, only making contact a few times, before getting irritated with himself. This resulting in him leaving the table and sitting on the couch. He told everyone he was full already. I know he had not consumed his normal amount of alcohol that day due to the holiday and he knew everyone would be around. (Still in the denial and hiding stage) Therefore he experienced the withdrawal symptoms throughout the majority of the day. Eventually I believe he told my mom he was sick and wanted to go home. They soon left and he went home to "take care" of his symptoms. There was another incident similar to this one. But now I started to know what the symptoms meant, I did not know though how life threatening they could be. Another time we were at my sister's house, but this time was a little different, my mom wasn't there, it was just me and my sister and her family. (Mom was at my house with my kids) We were trying to talk to my dad about what was going on with his addiction. I am not sure if we got into an argument or really remember what happened, but he left and walked home. I left shortly after. A few hours later my sister called me a little freaked out, she said dad was banging on her door wanting in. She said he was acting very strange and she was scared. I told her to let him in and I would be over immediately. As soon as I got there, I could see he was acting out of character. Kind of like the time before when I first saw him withdrawal. Except this time it was worse. He was very mad and could not control his body movements. I called a friend of mine who is a recovered alcoholic and told her what was going on. (I had confided in her before regarding my dad) She said he was withdrawing pretty badly and she would be right over. She and her husband live right around the corner so they got there pretty fast. As soon as they got there they went into intervention mode trying to get him to realize he needed help and to go with them. He of course refused and after less than an hour he was ready to leave. My friend agreed to take him home so he wouldn't have to walk and as soon as he got towards the refrigerator he opened it and grabbed an old bottle of wine that was half gone hidden in the back. He must have seen it when he was over earlier that evening and that's why he walked over. He tucked the bottle into his jacket protecting it like it was a newborn baby. My friend advised us to let it go for that moment because he was in such a severe desperate state and at that point into his addiction without the alcohol that night his body may not have made it through the symptoms.

If you noticed in the beginning his withdrawal symptoms did not start out that severe. Over time his body became more tolerant to the high amounts of alcohol, making his withdrawal more severe.

Denial

"When we deny we lie, and when we lie, life passes us by"

Denial is our minds unconscious defense in accepting our reality. I have learned that addicts can be very stubborn and most of the time in denial of their own addiction. Have you ever heard an addict say this?

- "I don't have a problem?"
- "It's not as bad as you think."
- "I can handle this."
- "Look at you, you're not perfect."
- "I can quit anytime I want."
- "I don't use (or drink) every day."
- "I'm not a junkie or crack head."
- "What do you think I am?"
- "I can stop whenever I want."

If you're nodding your head right now it's because you have heard one of these phrases or a similar one. At this point your addict is in the denial stage. This is one of the hardest stages to deal with. From my experience, the more you try to bring the addict out of their own denial; it seems to push them further away and often makes them angry at you. This can leave you feeling mad at yourself like you're not doing enough. This is the part of addiction that I believe will drive you crazy. You find yourself using all your strength and willpower to try and make the addict realize their own addiction. At least that's what I did. I focused on this denial stage every day, reading every book, searching numerous web pages, trying to talk to as many people that I knew for advice. I wanted a quick answer and an even quicker fix. This stage can be mentally and physically exhausting for both you and the addict. It can quickly cause additional stress and problems in your own personal life and even more stress in the life of the addict.

I was the roughest toughest guy around. I was the guy everyone was afraid to mess with. I could intimidate you with my voice and words. I could get any girl I wanted; they all loved the bad guy. I could also get anyone to do anything for me. I could do any drug and any amount and still hold my composure. So I thought. This was my denial. Everyone in my crowd looked up to me like I was their leader and their protector. I liked that feeling and that was another part of my denial. The fact that everyone around me never tried to help me caused my denial to run deep. The only ones who did try to help was my family, but I always blew them off. My so called friends used with me every day and gave me free drugs to keep me close to them. They did not know it was killing me and neither did I. I was in denial so deep I was losing my mind. The grip I had on my sanity was slipping quickly. I felt that I could not let anyone see me struggling. I did not want them to see me tormented and broken, not even my family. I did not want to lose the feeling of being looked up at and the feeling of my friends wanting to be around me. What I did not realize was that it was not me they wanted to be around, it was the drugs. My denial for my addiction and my head strong attitude was destroying my life.

After a tough battle and years later I overcame my denial of needing help. I realized this when I had completely lost my family and my friends had all dwindled away to other drug houses. My health was failing and I had no one to turn to. I realized all the things I had given up for my drugs. At that moment I realized I was not as tough as I thought. I was weak. I let a drug destroy my life, take away my family, and cause me to do things soberly I would have never done.

After overcoming the toughest realization of my life I now live my life sober and free. I have people that look up to me and respect me for the good in my life. I am still a leader, but my followers are people like me. They are sober and recovered. I am stronger and tougher now that I have been in my entire life. I owe it to sobriety for that.

Steven Chaney

Enable

"When you enable, an addict will never experience
the full effects of their addiction."

Enabling is the actions you take or do not take towards your addict, which allows them to continue using their drugs or alcohol without repercussions.

When I was told I was an enabler it was like a hard slap in the face. Here I was thinking I was doing all these things to help when in reality all I was doing was enabling my addict to use more freely and not to have to worry about responsibilities. The longer an addict uses and the worse it gets, the more the friends and families start to enable them. Doing so, we as non addicts start to become more stressed out and emotionally unstable ourselves. We start to do things for them that morally we know are wrong. We put up with more negative behavior and often compromise with the addict because we do not want them to hurt anymore or have any more stress in their life. We as non addicts will experience anxiety, hopelessness, fear, anger, and frustration. We experience many sleepless nights staying awake worrying and crying about our addict. This affects us emotionally and physically.

There are many ways a person can enable someone. Normally the person closest to the addict with the strongest relationship enables them the most. This is the spouse, parent or child of the addict. They are more on the defensive side and they enable continuously without even knowing it. Then there are the siblings and friends of the addict. They too enable the addict without seeing the truth from other people's eyes. Coworkers, distant relatives and other acquaintances enable as well, but they see more of what really is going on.

There are many ways we enable and not even notice it.

Have you ever rationalized your addict's behavior? Making excuses for them so they are more like the victim and allowing them to not be responsible for their actions.

Have you ever justified with the addicts because you want so badly to believe what they are saying?

Minimizing the problem is also very commonly done and the biggest in enabling. Acting like it is not as bad as it really is when you know it is out of control.

You take over the addicts responsibilities, thinking you are helping out by eliminating stress, but all you are really doing is allowing them to use more freely and not have to worry about everyday tasks. This also trains the addict to not take action when there is a stressful situation or task because they know you will step in and do it for them. Not allowing the addict to handle their own responsibilities or problems will affect them when trying to get them to help themselves with their addiction. They will expect you to do it all for them, since you had already taken over other obstacles in their life.

Blaming ourselves and the ones around the addict is the

hardest one I think. Pointing fingers and making excuses for an addicts behavior seems like the easy way out of the whole situation. All that does is make it hard for everyone and again allows the addict to play the victim role and not have to take responsibility for their addiction.

Being in complete denial of the addict's addiction allows the problem to be nonexistent. The addict knows they will never be confronted about it and will never have to face their reality. This allows them to use more comfortably and freely.

Trying to keep the peace between you and your addict is also a way of enabling. Avoiding problems and confrontations so you can keep your addict close to you only allows them to use without consequences because you have allowed them to not be accountable for their actions.

Have you ever done one of the following for your addict?

- Let them borrow money or gave it to them?
- Took care of their kids?
- Allowed them to stay in your home?
- Remained in a relationship with the active addict?
- Bought them food?
- Paid for their gas?
- Paid for their rent?
- Gave them rides due to them losing their license or car?
- Lie to others to cover up their problems?
- Supply a car for them to use without paying for it?
- Avoid social atmospheres with them?
- Argued continuously about the addiction without treatment being the goal?
- Bailed them out of jail?
- Cleaned up after the messes in their lives?
- Let them drive your car when you know they are driving drunk or under the influence of drugs?
- Ignore or make jokes about their problem?

- Do not confront them about their addiction?
- Knowingly pay for their alcohol or drugs?
- Allow an active addict to have custody of their children?
- Put yourself in a financial rut due to their addiction?
- Put yourself in physical harm?
- Fail to confront the main enabler in the addict's life?
- Use or drink with the addict?
- Felt obligated to bail them out of every situation because you felt sorry for them?
- Continually make excuses for them?
- Do everything for them because you think they are helpless?

I am sure you can name more ways you have enabled your addict, but these are few I know firsthand and have experience with.

When we enable an addict we are acting just like their drug or alcohol. We help take away their reality and help them ignore their feelings. In most cases the drug or alcohol is not even the main problem. It is their lack of ability to acknowledge their feelings and their fear of facing their problems.

Facing my fears and feeling my sadness is so much harder now; I do not have the drugs to numb me from my reality any more. Even though it is hard, I know that my feelings are real. I am alive and can start my journey to recovery.
Katie Herndon
Meth addict.

In the beginning I always made excuses for my dad and lied to people about his behaviors. I would lie that he was not drunk but really tired and had a long day, that's why he is slurring his words and stumbling. Or he has a speech problem and he is hard to understand. I would allow him to lie to my face and would not have the guts to call him out on it. He would lie about not drinking when I could smell it on his breath; he would blame it on his chewing gum or the cigar he just smoked. I felt that if I kept making him feel guilty about his lying and drinking it would make it worse, so I would play dumb and let him get away with the lies. By me feeling sorry for him and letting him get away with stuff with no repercussions I was enabling him. I would let him borrow my car so he could go to a job meeting that was supposed to take a few hours. After a few hours would pass, I would not hear from him. When he would bring my car back he would be so drunk he could not even stand up. I could not imagine how he even drove. One time he kept my car for a few days and every time I would ask for it he would make an excuse to have to use it again. I knew they were lies and he just needed my car for freedom because his car was broke, but again I enabled him. When I finally got my car back, there were a few dents on the door sides, alcohol was spilled on the passenger seat and a sprite container that smelled of vodka was in the console. I would always give my dad money, not a lot, a ten or twenty whenever he would ask. He would always say it was for gas money or help on a bill. Each time I gave him the money, I knew exactly what it was for, but how do you tell a parent no? I remember one time I had given him twenty dollars to go to the store with; I decided to follow him that day. He headed straight to the liquor store. I sat back for a minute and decided to text him. I asked him where he was and what he was doing. His reply was at the store buying groceries. Lie. And even though I knew it and was right there seeing it for my own eyes I let it go, thinking to myself, well if he needs it that bad I do not want to embarrass him or make him mad at me for following him. A big part of my enabling was I was so defensive towards my dad that I did not want to accept what was really happening, so if I just kept doing what I was doing maybe things would just miraculously get better. I enabled him by not allowing him to take responsibility for his addiction. I was hurting him more then I was helping him.

Being enabled by my family was killing me faster than I expected and I was not ready to die yet. I wanted them so badly to put their foot down to me, set strong boundaries and give me tough love. I needed to learn life on my own. Even though I would have thrown huge fits and started fights, I knew deep down inside what I needed. My family did not want to deal with the drama so they just gave me everything I asked for and needed to survive. This allowed me to feed my addiction freely. The longer they enabled me, the farther away I was from realizing how bad I really was. For almost 15 years my family dealt with my addiction as "my way of life" They thought they were doing me a favor but in reality they were helping me dig my own grave.

A 40 year old recovered alcoholic finally living life.

Sheldon Murphy

Rock bottom

"Not every addict has to hit their rock bottom to want to change, but in most it does play a big part in their life as an addict."

Rock bottom is a term commonly used in the life of an addict, and a term their friends and families may never understand.

For each person is different and so is their idea of being at their worst. Rock bottom is basically when the addict has lost everything and now realizes they need help. Trying to make an addict realize they have hit their rock bottom is not as easy as it sounds. Even though you can point out to them everything they have lost, and if they are not ready to accept the reality, they will deny they are at their worst. An addict will hold on to anything to try to prove they have not lost it all. They will try to justify every incident in their life and make excuses for the reasons they don't have what they once did. It's also a big part of the denial stage. I believe it will still help to try to make the addict realize the things they have lost, but it needs to be done in a loving way. An addict already has lost love and in their steps to get sober they need to feel love as much as they can. There is a difference in loving your addict with boundaries and loving your addict in an enabling way. Some call it tough love and in most cases it is the best kind of love.

When an addict does hit their rock bottom point they may

feel they are at their wits end and they now know the only thing left for them is death or help. They may feel pure emptiness at this point; confused, scared, helpless, depressed, they may already feel death even though they are still breathing. At rock bottom they will realize they have lost their friends and family and have no one to turn to.

At rock bottom an addict is at their weakest moment in their addiction and anything can happen at this point. If there is no one there to encourage the addict to get help and pour out the love and hope they so badly need, the addict may feel there is nothing left and ultimately take their own life. When the addict does decide to get help they need 100% support and encouragement. They have made the biggest step in their life to turn things around and to them this may be the scariest part.

If the addict is at their rock bottom and refuses help, they *will* eventually lose their life to their addiction.

In other situations an addict may realize their life is spiraling out of control and before they lose everything or reach their rock bottom they decide to change and get help.

In some situations an addict may not have the chance to reach their rock bottom. Death beat them to it. This happens more often than we like and unfortunately we are left with the guilt and sadness of not being able to intervene before it was too late.

When an addict has not hit their rock bottom stage it is very hard for the family and friends to cope. We want so badly for them to realize their addiction and the toll it has taken on their lives. We see what it has taken away and we do not understand how they can live the way they are. But what we need to realize is that once someone becomes an addict they adapt to the lifestyle. Adapting themselves to their new lifestyle they do not notice the things they have lost or given up because they are replaced with new things in their new life as an addict. Being under the influence of their drug or alcohol they are able to dull their emotions and memories. Doing so, they do not realize the reality they are in and how bad they are living their life. If the addict is surrounded by other addicts they will feed off each other's misery and often try to comfort each other. It is also harder for them to want change, especially when they see the ones around them who are giving them "empty love" not changing and continually using. There are no positive relationships between addicts under the influence.

.

It took me 7 years to hit my rock bottom. I had lost everything, my wife, kids, home and my sanity. I will never forget the day I woke up from my empty bottle and saw my reflection in the mirror. I barely recognized myself. I saw a man who once had everything and now sat with nothing. That very moment I realized that I could not live the rest of my life like this. I was drowning and needed a life jacket and that life jacket was myself. I made a promise to myself that day to get sober and get my life back. It was like something just clicked in me and I knew I could do it. I believed in myself.

A recovered alcoholic enjoying my second chance at life,

On the Outside Looking In – Surviving The Blind Side of Addiction
Mathew Towsend

<u>Detoxification</u>

Detox is the first step in overcoming an addiction to drugs and alcohol. Your body has to rid itself of the substance it has become so addicted and dependent on.

While detoxing an addicts can experience extreme convulsions, delirium, tremors, shakes, rapid heart rate, loss of appetite, excessive sweating, visual hallucinations, delusions, disorientation, and insomnia.

It is very important an addict seeks a professional to help them through the detox process. This process can be very life threatening and without the proper treatment an addict can lose their life while in the process of trying to regain it all back.

Almost every addict has to experience some sort of detox in order to start their life over being sober. Some experience it with the help of a medical team and professionals. Others are not so lucky and have to experience this nightmare on their own in jail or in their home by themselves, praying that they can make it through.

Imagine your body being highly addicted to something and then all of a sudden you take it away. In some cases an addict will have to use a little each day, lessening their drug or alcohol as the days pass, to slowly wean their bodies off. That way they do not experience the heightened results of the detox. Alcohol and heroin are the two worst substances to detox off of. With heroin you are sick for days, throwing up uncontrollably, unable to eat, pain all throughout your body. I remember hearing a girl coming off heroin in the detox center. It was heart breaking, she screamed for help and cried desperately, but there was nothing any one could do for her. She had to go through the detox to get better.

Going through detox was hard. What I learned though is you have to feel through your emotions. I was very scared during my detox, not having my drug I had to deal with my body and the way it felt. It was an experience I will never forget and also never want to experience again. My detox was my moment of truth. When I realized what my body had to go through just get rid of the drugs I was drowning myself with was surreal.

I did not detox alone, I went to a detox facility and without them I know I would not have made it. They kept me positive and kept me hopeful. I am so thankful today that I am alive and sober. The one thing that keeps me going the most is looking back at my years of addiction and never wanting to experience all the pain and heartache again.

Teresa Liam

January 27th is the day my dad realized he needed to reach out to us and ask for help. My mom came over that evening to get out of the house due to his heavy drinking that day. It was late evening about nine. My husband and I were getting ready for bed, kids were asleep and mom was in the spare room resting. My phone rang and it was my dad. I quickly answered and he could barely talk. I remember hearing him gasping for air as he was trying to scream. He finally got out that he needed to go to the emergency room; he was having a heart attack. I jumped up, told my mom to stay and watch the kids and that my husband and I would go get him. I stayed on the phone with him until we got to his house. I was nervous to go in, so my husband went in to get him. He had to hold him up as he walked him to the truck. I called the hospital that works closely with a detox and treatment facility. The hospital was about 20 minutes away but I knew if we could get him there, there would be a good chance of him getting admitted into the detox hospital. The drive there seemed like it took forever, I stayed on the phone with the ER nurse letting her know his status, which at that point was not good. He could not sit in the seat and he kept falling forward into the front of the truck. (We sat him in the backseat.) He kept screaming for us to hurry and grabbing his chest, his face was red and sweaty and he could barely hold his head up. He kept groaning and making weird noises as he was flopping around going with the motion of the truck. We finally made it to the ER and the nurses were there waiting with a wheel chair. They quickly wheeled him in as I went to the registration booth to get him signed in. About an hour passed and they called us back. We were told he was not having a heart attack, (thank God) but he had experienced a severe anxiety attack, associated with all the effects from alcohol withdrawal. Even though he was experiencing withdrawal symptoms, his blood alcohol level was still above the legal limit. They gave him something to calm him down and an IV to get him some liquids. He was severely dehydrated. They also gave him a catheter so he wouldn't have to get up. The nurse from the detox hospital was there and was a little familiar with my dad's situation. (Another time before it got this bad, we had tricked him to go there to try to get him in treatment, he refused at that time.) She was a very sweet lady and knew how to talk to him. After a few hours of being in the hospital he sobered up a little. After talking to him and pouring our hearts out to him about getting better and getting help, he came out of his denial stage and finally accepted the fact that yes, he had a major problem and it was not going to ever go away if he did not get help. He also now understood after the scare that he had just gone through that his life was in danger and he could die from this. I felt like a kid on Christmas morning after hearing him agree to go to the detox center. We quickly filled out the paper work before he could change his mind and a van from the facility came to pick him up.

It was about three in the morning when he got transported. We were exhausted. We were not allowed to go with him or follow them to the treatment center. This allowed the doctors to evaluate him and get him set up with no distractions.

Later that morning I called to check on his status; the nurse there was very nice and agreed to talk with me on the phone. At first she tried to sugarcoat how he was doing and I could tell she was trying not to tell me something. I asked her to please be honest with me and that I needed to know in detail what was going on. At that point she got very serious with me and told me that the detox that my dad was experiencing was the worst she had ever seen with alcohol. They had to heavily sedate him shortly after he arrived. He was experiencing full body convulsions that he could not control. He was also in a lot of pain and his blood pressure was at a very unsafe level. His anxiety and stress were also extremely elevated. They put him in a room where they could watch him closely and checked on him every 15 minutes. The first full day he was there he was unable to leave his room due to being overly medicated. I went to go see him that night and got him to take a shower and brought him a robe, slippers, new socks and underwear.

He was in a nice area until they realized he was uninsured so the next day they moved him to the lower floor; less privacy, but the nurses were still very nice.

The second day I went a little earlier around lunch time. He was better than the day before, but still experienced the shakes and was still medicated. There is a room that everyone can sit in and watch T.V, so we sat in there and just had small talk. He had not eaten anything but a few pieces of lettuce since arriving at the detox center. His stomach was very bloated and he did not have an appetite. Visiting with him in this condition was strange, but I enjoyed being able to talk to him for the most part.

The third day my mom and I went to visit. This day his spirits were so much better. He was able to focus on us and I watched him and my mom laugh and talk amongst themselves; not something I had seen in a long time. They were both enjoying each other's company. We sat again in the room and played hang man with the rest of the people there. He was still heavily medicated, but he had eaten a full breakfast that morning and was starting to drink more water. The nurses said he was their favorite patient there and they loved his funny sense of humor. Since he had become more coherent they started him on some counseling that day. He attended a group meeting and then group therapy that night. I talked to him on the phone after and he really enjoyed the classes he had taken. He was enjoying the positive atmosphere and he felt accepted there.

January 31st, the fourth day he was there, I received a phone call early that morning that they were releasing him today at one. He was not even there three full days. I was shocked, just when he started to come around they were ready to move him out. Why? Because he was self-pay and could not afford it. I knew this was not a good idea, I knew he needed more time there to get completely sober and receive more therapy. When I went to pick him up I could tell he was not ready and was scared to face his reality. They sent him home with a prescription for high blood pressure, anxiety medication and pain medication

When released from the detox center he was not given advice, resources or education on how to stay sober or how to get counseling. All he knew at this point was addiction. He had lost his normal way of life. His problems still existed when he got home. The feelings of shame and guilt of how he was living and what he had done to his life was haunting him. For a few days after leaving the detox facility he was so weak, he did not get out of his bed. I would bring him breakfast in the morning and help him take the blood pressure medication they prescribed him. I could tell he was confused and did not know what to do next. He wanted to live the normal life he did before, but he did not know where to begin. Without having the proper treatment he so badly needed, he relapsed February 11th, 11 days after leaving the detox center. He started out with just a little bit of alcohol at a time then he went back to guzzling a fifth of vodka every day and night.

Overdose

Overdose is a very serious and scary situation when an adverse reaction happens due to drug or alcohol use. Overdose can lead to long term medical issues and death.

First of all, do not wait until it is too late; call 911 as soon as you see or hear someone's life is in danger. At this point time is precious and this person is depending on you for your quick action and smart thinking. Do not be afraid of getting in trouble if you are a using with this person either. Their life is more important than a "slap on the wrist." Could you imagine the guilt of not calling for help because you were scared, then this person dies?

When someone starts to overdose it can take their life quickly and or cause lifelong effects on their brain and bodies. Signs of overdose can include:

- Slow and faint breathing
- Fingertips and lips turn blue
- They are lethargic and unresponsive when you shake them or try to communicate with them
- Sweating
- Body shaking
- Rapid pulse
- Rapid eye movement
- Vomiting
- Foaming at the mouth
- Pressure or tightness the chest
- Heart attack, stroke, or seizure
- No breathing at all
- No pulse
- Unable to talk or walk

Anyone can overdose; it does not matter how long you have been using or how high your tolerance is. Yes, you can overdose the very first time you experiment with drugs and alcohol. The more you mix drugs and alcohol together the greater your risk of overdosing. Your weight, overall health, potency of your drug and alcohol, and any underlying illness you may have, all play a factor in overdosing.

I remember being at my first high school party my freshman year. The party was already out of control. Kids of all ages were drunk or high on some drug. I remember a bunch of people crowded by the bathroom door screaming at this one kid to get up and to quit joking around. They were all laughing and making stupid jokes about this kid. I did not understand what was going on so I made my way through the crowd and realize the kid on the floor was overdosing. It was horrifying. No one around him was helping; they were all too drunk themselves. This kid was lying on the floor with white foam drooling out of his mouth and all I could think of was why is no one doing anything? In the midst of all this chaos, I could see kids still laughing and partying, knowing this kid was in the bathroom dying. I quickly went in the other room and called 911. Since no one else seemed to care, I did not want to be the freshman who crashed the party because of the kid in the bathroom. I knew the cops and paramedics would be there quick so I exited the party. I stayed close so I could watch. After a few minutes of being there they carried him out on a stretcher. The party was broken up and many kids were given citations for underage drinking. Lots of parents were called that night and many kids got into trouble. I did not care though. If it was not for me being there that night that boy would have died. There was not one level headed person at that party to make the right decision. I later found out around school that he had taken painkillers and was drinking alcohol. I had a class with him, but I never said anything about what happened. I always wondered if he knew how lucky he was that I was there that night.

Mike Freeman

<u>Intervention</u>

I wish I knew more about intervention when we were at our breaking point. I tried to do my research, but it seemed every place I called they were too expensive or did not give me the information on how to get help with the intervention process.

Not knowing the facts, I tried to put together my own intervention which did not go as planned, as most "at home" interventions go. We did not know the proper guidelines, say the right things or approach the situation the way we were supposed to. All the things we wanted to say we could not because our emotions got in the way and we did not have a mediator to help guide us through the intervention process. We did not even have a rehab set up if he decided to change. We were completely unprepared. That resulted in emotional chaos between everyone involved, arguments, and in the end nothing was achieved. I highly recommend hiring a professional before ever trying to intervene in this manner.

The intervention process is not as simple as often thought of or as it sometimes appears on the recent television show. It's important when considering an intervention, to keep these crucial steps in mind. The basics are to always hire a professional, someone who has not only worked in the field for a few years, but also holds a counseling license or certification in addiction, and / or certification as an interventionist - CIS or a BRI . Call the interventionists company or private consultant and ask questions. Look for an interventionist and or intervention company that quotes a minimum success rate of 85% or higher. I can't say it enough... Take time to research.

Often, I am called to a job where the family has previously attempted the intervention themselves. They had brought someone in locally who has worked in the field of addiction (but has not been trained in the Intervention process) or brought in someone they know is in recovery to help them. An intervention is not a 12 step call and it's not a negotiation. Addiction, alcoholism, and the family dynamics surrounding addiction, have many components that must be better understood by the family and friends before pursuing an intervention, and that requires a professional. Without a professional the process usually fails. This means the professional has to face some unnecessary negative mindsets, regroup and re frame the family from the old ways and build the new process.

When families are in crisis, which is usually the point at which an intervention becomes a reality, people tend to let their emotions take over. That decision making hinders smart choices when choosing an interventionist as well as a treatment center. Even though it feels you're in the middle of a crisis, be open to taking time to do a little research and ask questions. Be prepared to take time, breathe and get organized. You can make a huge difference if you take time to get educated on the professionals process.

Think about timing; what's the best time to get everyone together (important people may need time to drive or even fly in). If you are talking to a company, ask to speak with the interventionist before hiring anyone. Arrange timing so you can meet with the interventionist before the actual family day process with all the participants. Ask questions share all your information and be open to the interventionist's guidance.

Although I am mentioning a lot of timing components, it is also important to remember you cannot control everything... and if you try you will never do this. You will have time to do more and you will have help doing it, once you hire the interventionist. In the meantime, consider these points, do the best you can and then move forward - don't wait for the perfect time! When you have done your research and hired a professional, trust them. Try to get as many people involved as possible (the old tendency is to keep the family secret- you need to step out of that old mindset). Remember, if no one changes, nothing changes!

Intervention process choices:

There are a few models of intervention that families can

research online to see which model they feel most comfortable with, but REMEMBER - the old ways get the same old results. The main models are: The Systematic, The Smart, The Invitational, and the Johnson Model. Although most interventionists tend to follow one set model, I believe an interventionist should be educated in all models. In my 18 years as a professional working in addictions, I have found it important to not only be educated in all the models but to also utilize the best of all models, when necessary. I believe a good interventionist, will base that decision on the family dynamics, a review of the situation once they have met with the family and on into a quick review and ability to think on their feet while the intervention process is in action. In my practice, I find utilizing the Systematic and Smart models to be the most successful. Here the family is prepared through education on addiction, manipulations, enabling and how to approach the loved one with caring assertive love. Families need to understand it's not a quick fix and I always encourage them to step out of crisis mode and into a process of learning, be open to taking time to organize the group of people involved, being ready to take a minimum of 5 hours for everyone to come together for family day and participate in the learning process. Family day is a day to prepare everyone participating. This is done by educating, role playing, helping them review and understand why their current way has not been working, learning support by building new responses and behaviors that encourage and support the family into a new way - a shift into recovery for themselves also. The process also includes loving assertive letter writing approach, how to deal with the objections they may be presented with, and if necessary, how to shift into a tough love status. Family day is a time to not only review and learn each component of the process but to become comfortable in each step. Throughout the process the participants follow the interventionist training and lead to guide the process into the necessary shift. The typical process can take 20 minutes, up to into three to four hours and even during times of tough love possibly days before your loved one goes into treatment, although the average is just a couple hours.

I often describe the intervention process to families as a dance... The family has to learn new life steps when dealing with addiction and although the dance may feel awkward at first, they must trust the process. Then the preparations help you dance into the process as you talk from a heartfelt place with your caring letters. Share with your loved one the joy of having them in your life, the pain of watching alcoholism/ addiction tear their lives apart and the "gift" you want to offer them to get them out of the problem and send them into a new life solution. The letters are the most powerful part of the process. If needed, after the letter reading, the group is trained to "verbally dance". To further address and break through any additional denial; to dance around long enough for the loved one to see the need and necessity of shifting. That dance may involve various shifts from loving tears, denial, to angry words, manipulative behaviors, to sad tears and silence, back to loving tears and ultimately to the acceptance of

95

help. The key is "no one shifts" and "no one negotiates". Trust and follow the plan. Throughout the process, participants need to trust the interventionist, stay on task, and remember that in order to insure they get their loved one to accept help, denial must be broken and the loved one needs to feel completely helpless so they reach out and accept the help being offered. They need to feel that treatment is the ONLY way to gain back their life.... because in reality... it is!

That's what helps the one being intervened on - to dance into a breakthrough of their denial, and to a new truth. A truth that supports them in the decision that I not only have to shift, but I accept the reality that I "need" help, I "need" to shift. In my opinion, if you really want to help your loved one, then an intervention is your solution. If you really want a successful intervention, then it's imperative to bring a professional interventionist in to help you reach that goal.

While choosing the interventionist, you also want to feel confident in your choice of treatment center. I am always saddened and frustrated to have a successful intervention process, get the person to treatment and then within days begin to receive frustrating calls from the family regarding their unhappiness with the center they choose. They realize they did not research and ask questions. They didn't know the right questions to ask. Just as before, there are crucial questions to ask when considering a treatment center. Some question to consider may include is insurance a possibility, does insurance cover detox and treatment. What is the length of coverage? What is the length of stay? Ideally, a six to sixteen week program can be crucial to building a strong foundation. The longer they stay, the more education they receive. Longer time to address a variety of issues, and you increase the chances of a higher success rate for your loved one. What model of treatment do they offer? Some models to review are the Disease or Twelve Step model, Spiritual or Christian based model, Personal Motivation or Scientology model. Additional questions to ask treatment centers regarding the client's services are if they offer individual or group counseling? BOTH are important. Are the counselors certified or licensed and are those state or national certifications / licenses (some centers claim their counselors are certified but actually they are certified through the center itself, not a state recognized certification.) Inquire about success rate, but know that when a center quotes a success rate they are usually referring to length of stay at their center, not long term success. A long- term success rate is hard to track but good aftercare and support system referrals are the key to success after completion.

Aftercare options should include two or more of the following. Arranging to see an addictions counselor for at least one year after treatment, hiring a sober companion or Reintegration Coach to be there immediately upon the clients return to home. Their services should extend from three days to two weeks. This is an excellent adjunct to helping your loved one to comfortably begin to implement the tools and relapse prevention plan learned in treatment. Going to meetings, Smart Recovery, 12

Step, and or Faith based recovery meetings, participating in intensive after care classes, drug monitoring or case management programs. All are excellent support systems and show increased success rates into long term recovery for those who commit to maintaining and building their recovery process. Recovery is a lifelong process; a strong foundation begins with entering a good treatment center and then extending that process into a strong aftercare support system(s)

"There is a solution to the chaos and insanity that addiction brings into your life."

Patricia Peters, BA, LAC, CADC II, BRI-I

Life Skills Counselor/ Interventionist/ Intensive Personal Growth Workshop Facilitator and Public Speaker

I have worked in the field of Addictions and Social Services for over 18 years addressing issues of Addictions, Dual Diagnosis, Life Skills and Co-Dependency. www.Steppingintochange.com

What I did learn through intervention is how important it is to write letters to your addict. With the letter writing you are given the chance to express your true feelings. The letters also give you a guide for what you are trying to say. Letters are forever, unlike conversations. You can always go back and reread letters and get a better understanding of what someone is trying to say to you. People tend to listen better when someone is reading a letter rather than babbling and everyone jumping in on a conversation. To learn more about letter writing and interventions please contact an intervention service.

3

Alcohol

A feeling I will never forget

February 22, 2008 will be a day I will never forget. A day that I felt every emotion imaginable, from anger, to a feeling of pure sadness, confusion, abandonment, rage, emptiness, serenity, peace, and ironically a feeling of hope. Even though I did not sleep very well that night, (which was normal for me) I woke up that morning and felt well rested. That night before and years prior, have been emotionally, mentally and physically exhausting with many unanswered questions. Although with everything that was going on I still put a smile on my face. I also still did all my motherly duties, household duties, took care of our family business, and my hairstylist job. My days were full of stress and emotionally I was drained (I am most certain that everyone else around me and my family were too). My own anxiety of not knowing what was happening was getting the best of me. Fearing the phone calls I would receive and the situations I would be in. The fear of the unknown weighed heavily in my heart and in my mind every morning, day and night. This particular morning I got up, made coffee, said good morning to my mom who had stayed with us that night, got my son ready for pre-school, said good bye to my husband as he left for work and kissed my sleeping baby girl on the cheek. I tried to keep everyday feeling as normal as possible so my kids and even my husband would not feel the personal chaos that I was going through. Strangely though, throughout that morning I felt a little at ease. Not a feeling I had felt in years and definitely not a feeling I had experienced in the months coming up to this day. I remember like it was yesterday. That day on February 22nd around 11am I was walking into the bathroom to finish getting dressed to go to work. As I made it to the doorway of the bathroom, suddenly I had the urge to stop walking. A strong sensation come over me, all of a sudden I felt an instant sense of peace and it was almost like I could feel a release of sadness and tension leaving my body. My mind felt so relaxed and stress free, like I was floating in the clouds. It was a moment of pure serenity. The world around me seemed to be still and I couldn't tell if there was action or any commotion going on. It was like I had stepped out of my body. I don't remember hearing anything at all, complete silence. I also do not remember seeing the walls around me, it was like I knew I was there in my house standing in the bathroom doorway, but it did not feel like I was there at all. I felt like I had a haze over my eyes and everything was kind of dull. My body felt somewhat numb and my mind euphoric like. I stood there in the doorway of the bathroom being over powered by this feeling, and even though I was enjoying it, I was also a little scared of it. I am not sure how long the feeling lasted, it felt like an eternity. As quickly as the feeling came over me it left just as quick. It is a feeling I will never forget and believe I will never experience again. I walked into the bathroom and stared at myself in the mirror, confused about what just happened. I couldn't help but to think hard, trying to analyze the feeling I had just experienced.

Thinking in the back of my mind that with everything that's been going on, why all of a sudden would I feel so calm? Maybe my mind and body was at a breaking point and this was its way of giving me a relaxing moment, before I had a nervous breakdown.

The rest of the morning felt a little off, something just did not seem right, but strangely again, I felt very calm and at ease. I got to work around 12:30 and did my first appointment. My first client was a haircut so it took me about 30 minutes to finish her. After she had paid and re booked her next appointment, I went back to my station to clean up before my next appointment arrived.

The phone at our salon rings constantly (which is a good thing) and the next phone call was for me. Whoever answered yelled for me to get the phone (thinking it was a client to book an appointment) so I went to the phone....

"Hi can I help you?"

It was my brother in law. "Hey, are you with a client?"

I answered no and I could tell something wasn't right, the way his voice sounded abnormally deep, very serious and also somewhat shaky. My mind started racing. I knew in my heart something was terribly wrong. What he told me next has drastically changed my life forever....

Alcohol facts and history

What comes to your mind when you hear the word alcohol?
For some it's a mixed drink, like a vodka soda or a jack and coke.
Others may hear alcohol and associate it with a time to party and
get wasted. A time to mingle with friends drinking everything from
beer, wine, hard liquor and even doing keg stands. Some hear the
word alcohol and think about meeting up with friends for happy
hour at a local restaurant or bar to enjoy a few cocktails. Addicts
may hear the word alcohol and think of it as their way of escaping
reality, or that alcohol is their worst enemy.

When we hear the word alcohol we most likely cringe and
think of all the devastation and torment it has caused in our life.
When we see others enjoying alcohol we may think negative
thoughts because we are reminded of how it destroyed our lives
and our loved ones.

Even if we enjoy small beverages for ourselves every now
and then we know firsthand the severe negative side of alcohol.

I believe alcohol is overly advertised as a feel good drink.
While watching T.V it is on many commercials being advertised as
fun, beautiful, and glamorous. When you go to a restaurant it is the
first thing you are offered, even if you're an adult eating dinner
with your kids. The drink specials are recited to you right after
your waiter greets your table or the menu is already open to the
alcohol section. The sad part is that waiter does not know if you

have just lost someone due to alcohol, currently struggling with alcohol addiction, or living on the blind side of someone's alcohol addiction. It automatically sets a mood, whether it is annoyance because you are constantly reminded that alcohol is not always a feel good drink or an addict that may become uncomfortable if they are still struggling with saying no when offered a drink.

When you think of alcohol do you really know anything about it? Where exactly did it come from? What is it made of? What is really going on in our bodies as we consume alcohol? What are the facts of alcohol? Can alcohol kill you?

Alcohol is a mixture of ethanol and water that is usually 95 percent ethanol.

It is a derivative that comes from fermented fruits and grains. After the natural stages occur in the fruits and grains it then excretes the alcohol and carbon dioxide.

People soon discovered the effects that the fermented fruits and grains had on them. They enjoyed this so much that they organized a way to make alcohol.

No single country has been documented as the origin of alcohol. All ancient cultures are said to have discovered fermentation in some form or another.

In early America many consumed alcohol. Laws were created to ward against drinking excessively and being drunk. People looked down on the ones who drank and got drunk, especially when there were jobs to be done and children to take of.

These people were known as the "town drunkards"

(Alcohol in America, 2005).

I have put together a time line of events that I thought were very interesting about the laws of alcohol.

1697- New York created the law that all saloons must be closed and no alcohol sales will be made on Sundays.

1735- Georgia began the first state wide prohibition. (Prohibition was a legal act against alcohol manufacture, transportation and sale)

1742- Prohibition in Georgia completely failed.

1861-1865 No laws were made during the civil war against alcohol. Alcohol was used as an anesthesia for the soldiers and they drank it before it was time to fight.

1880- The Women's Christian Temperance Union otherwise known as WCTU was formed. This allowed the control of alcohol to be more powerful.

1900- By this time more than half the states had become dry and desperate people realized they could use the postal service to mail alcohol to dry states.

1913- The dry states soon caught on to the mailing of alcohol so they passed the Interstate Liquor Act. This made it illegal to mail alcohol to a dry state.

1917- The 18th amendment came into effect. This banned the sale and manufacture of alcohol.

1919- Volstead Act was passed. This act banned all forms of alcohol with a 1/2% content.

(Oracle Think Quest, 2005).

1920- National Prohibition took effect.

1933- Congress proposed the twenty-first Amendment and ended Prohibition

(*Wikipedia*, 2012).

1934- Original ABC Act (alcoholic beverage control) created the age limit law of 21 for alcohol sale and consumption.

1957- The American Medical Association declared alcoholism as a disease.

1974- Legal Drinking Age (LDA) for beer only lowered from 21 to 18.

1981- LDA kept the age limit 18 for on premise drinking, but changed off-premise drinking to 19.

1983- LDA passed all alcohol sales for beer at age 19 and up.

1985- Persons born on or after July 1st, 1966 can purchase and consume beer, wine, and liquor after their 21st birthday.

1987- LDA finalized 21 as the legal age to buy and consume all alcoholic beverages

(Virginia Department of Alcoholic Beverage Control, 1997-2012).

Today you will notice dry towns or cities are becoming more popular. The town I live in is very wet; you can find a liquor store or a store that sales liquor and beer on every corner. There is also a bar on each side of town and or a restaurant that has a liquor license. The number of liquor stores and bars we have accommodate the towns around us that are dry; a majority of the people that live in the "dry areas" travel to my town to buy or consume liquor. There are some pubs in the dry towns that serve alcohol, but to do so they must take a copy of everyone's driver's license upon entering their facilities.

Alcohol Statistics

Here are some alcohol statistics I thought were interesting.

- Over 15 million Americans suffer from alcohol dependency.
- Each year a young person is exposed to over 1,000 commercials for beer, wine coolers and several thousand fictional drinking incidents on television.
- In the United States every 30 minutes someone is killed in an alcohol related traffic accident.
- Each year the liquor industry spends almost 2 billion dollars on advertising and encouraging the consumption of alcoholic beverages.
- Americans spend over 90 billion dollars on alcohol each year.
- Each year students spend 5.5 billion dollars on alcohol, more than what they spend on soft drinks, tea, milk, juice, coffee, and books combined.
- 56% of students between grades 5th to 12th say alcohol related advertising encourages them to drink.
- Children who start drinking in their early teen years are more likely to become addicted.
- Alcohol is more toxic then many other drugs because it impacts the entire body not just the brain.
- Alcohol is the number 1 drug problem in America.
- About 1 out of 4 Americans admitted to general hospitals are undiagnosed from the effects of their alcohol addiction.
- Americans spend at least 100 million dollars a year on alcohol related problems.
- 4 out of 10 violent offenders report alcohol as a factor.
- (Alcohol Statistics, 2003-2012).

Effects of alcohol

As the evening comes around you begin to pick out your favorite outfit; the one that enhances all your physical features. You apply your makeup with perfection and your hair looks salon finished. The guys are adding their final touches with cologne, hair gel and their favorite graphic tee. Everyone's physical appearance is ready for a long night of partying, socializing and drinking.

What you did not prepare for or even think about is what is going to happen to your body internally as you indulge yourself tonight with alcohol.

The night has just begun and the laughter is all around you. You order your first drink.

The moment the alcohol enters your body the effects begin. First is the obvious taste. Whether it is a fruity cocktail, a strong tongue biting whiskey/bourbon, a cold beer or a shot that will make the hair on your head stand up, your mouth is the first to experience alcohol. Next is the throat, as the alcohol streams down towards your stomach it has already begun to enter your blood stream. The alcohol is now being carried through your body to your brain attacking your brain cells. As you continue to drink more, your coordination is being effected and your brain function is now beginning to deteriorate. As the night progresses your clothes, hair, and makeup still look flawless but internally you are starting to lose your perfection.

At this point you begin to slur your speech, your body

movements become delayed and less controlled. You are unaware of this and continue to drink more. Your choice of judgment and personal morals are now being effected. You are more talkative with strangers, and more flirtatious. You may stumble or sway back and forth. Unknowingly the alcohol has now made its way to your heart. As it travels through your blood vessels it causes them to relax to allow more blood flow through your skin and tissues. This results in a drop in your blood pressure. This drop can be dangerous for many. The body reacts to this drop by increasing its heart rate to allow for the blood to pump faster to its vital organs. This may cause your breathing to speed up. Now you can feel the effects of the alcohol, you feel a burst of energy throughout your body. You want to dance and be more social, but as you indulge in this new energy you quickly run out of breath and become worn out. You feel a little shaky inside, but you ignore these feelings because you are having fun. As you begin to drink more, the alcohol starts to act like a depressant on your central nervous system. This lowers your heart rate, your respiration lowers and so does your blood pressure. If dropped too low or too quick, this can be fatal. As the alcohol settles in your stomach it begins to irritate your stomach lining. This can cause a burning sensation or bloating. The alcohol is now blocking any absorption of essential vitamins and minerals that your body needs. Now all your body is absorbing is the alcohol. The alcohol is also being absorbed in your small intestines. You're still enjoying yourself with your friends, still unaware of what is really going on with your body and the negative effects that have already taken place. All you're worried about is applying more lip gloss and making sure your hair is in perfect place.

And the night goes on........

Now the alcohol is being metabolized in your liver. Your skin is also feeling the effects of the alcohol absorption. The blood flow is intense causing your skin to look flush and you may feel warm and tingly. Your internal organs and skin become dehydrated. You begin to feel parched and thirsty, but not for alcohol, so you order water.

Your lungs have also absorbed the alcohol excreting about 5% of the alcohol as you breathe. You can taste it in your mouth and smell it on your friend's breath.

The longer the alcohol gets absorbed in your body; different effects start to take place. Without you knowing it, your blood has now carried the alcohol to every part of your body. As it continually gets carried to your brain and your brain absorbs it, it dissolves into water inside your brain. This results in loss of inhibition and an aggressive feeling can be created. Even though you have consumed a little water your entire body is now becoming dehydrated including your brain cells causing damage to your organs. Your kidneys are working harder to help create urine from the alcohol it has absorbed.

As the night is coming to an end you are feeling all the effects the alcohol is having on your body.

As you get home you start to think about the night you just

had. Not about what is going on with your body, but about the friends, conversations and laughter you enjoyed physically, mentally and emotionally, not once thinking about how your internal body is suffering. Even though you have stopped drinking by now, the alcohol continues to deteriorate and deplete your body as it lowers your blood sugar levels. As you lay down, you start to feel dizzy and nauseous. As you fall asleep your body's central nervous system is being depressed and everything is working in slow motion. This can be very dangerous, especially if you have any underlying medical issues or have consumed more than your body can handle. Your brain cells that are now damaged and dehydrated are now creating your headache, otherwise known as your hangover. As the next day comes around, your concentration, memory and coordination are now affected as your body tries to recoup after a long night of drinking.......

Excess alcohol consumption can lead to liver disease. During the breakdown process of the alcohol in your liver it creates acetaldehyde. This is a by-product from the alcohol and can be more toxic to your body than the alcohol itself. In time this can attack your liver and cause cirrhosis. In a short amount of time, heavy drinking will cause your organs to swell and become inflamed.

After prolonged alcohol consumption in men there is a decline in their testosterone levels and their testicles begin to shrink, causing impotency. In women it can disrupt their menstrual

113

cycle and affect their fertility.

Overtime alcohol can cause severe depression, lethargy, anemia and anxiety. Your heart can develop an irregular heartbeat. This causes ineffective pumping of the blood from the heart and can create clots. These clots can travel to the brain and cause a stroke. Your brain can also have permanent damage affecting the nerve cells. Heavy and chronic drinking causes high blood pressure leading to many health risks and death.

Now that you know what alcohol really does to your body, the next time you go out, will you focus on just your physical appearance?

Mixing alcohol with medication and the side effects

Many people who take prescription and over the counter drugs consume alcohol. Interactions can cause negative side effects and can be fatal.

These are some common drugs people take and the effects of mixing them with alcohol.

- Acetaminophen- Can cause liver damage.

- Ibuprofen- Can cause ulcers and internal bleeding.

- Antidiabetics- Can cause stomach ache, vomiting, cramps, headaches, and low blood sugar.

- Anti-seizure- Can cause drowsiness.

- Codeine and Morphine- Can cause slow breathing, depress nervous system and drop blood pressure.

- Aspirin- Can cause stomach ulcers or internal bleeding

- Antidepressants- May cause extreme drowsiness

- Hormonal birth control- Can create blood clots and cause heart attack

(Coon *et al,* 1998).

My son was not your typical child. At the age of one he could count to ten, by the time he learned to walk he was always on the go, learning new things and getting into everything. He was a "momma's boy" and proud of it. I remember when I would pick him up from day care he would run to me with open arms. As he got older he was always here ready to help me with groceries and even house work. No matter where he went, he always made new friends. He cared deeply about other people and always tried to make others laugh when they were sad. He had a big heart and would never hurt a fly. In school he was the smartest in his class. He often got in trouble for talking out and was sent to the office. When I spoke with his teacher about it, she said he would always yell out the answers. To me that is no reason to send someone to the office. I asked my son why he would yell out the answers and he said the teacher would never call on him. I asked the teacher why and she said "she knew he would always have the right answer" So in other words because he was smart he was ignored. My son also had ADHD. RJ never lied, if he did get in trouble or did something wrong, he always confessed to it and told the truth. No one knew how to react to this and handle him. My son did what most the boys did growing up. He was in boy scouts, played baseball, football, and he went to summer camps. He was very musically inclined. He learned how to play the drums when he was 8 and by 12 he had taught himself by ear how to play the guitar and the piano. RJ and I had a great mother-son relationship; we used to talk about everything. I would tell him all the time how much I loved him and how much I believed in him. I wished he believed in himself the way I did. He did not see all the great things I saw in him. He used to tell me that he wanted to be normal like everyone else, but what was normal? A thug like everyone else, was that what he thought was normal?

RJ was in the Young Marines and wanted to serve in the Corps. This was his dream ever since he was a little boy and played with his little plastic army men. When he got into high school, that dream changed. A lot of things changed as he got older. When he was 15 I found out he was smoking pot and drinking. I was going through a divorce at this time and things were changing. I talked to my son and told him I did not like him smoking pot or drinking. He did not stop.

My son was wise beyond his years, when you spoke to him you had to speak on a different level; no one understood him. I think as he got older he just gave up on his ambitions and wanted so badly to be like everyone around him, like he felt out of place for being smarter than the others. My son never asked for anything and he would give you the shirt off his back. He was not an angel though; he gained the attitude that if you asked him not to do something it would make him want to do it even more, like every kid at that age, even I did that as a teenager.

When RJ was 17, I found out he was taking pills. Like any mother I wanted to stop him. I took him to a rehab that was five hours away, so no one could pick him up. After I dropped him off I thought this is it. Soon I will have my son back. Two days later I

117

got the phone call he had signed himself out and I needed to come pick him up.

The drinking continued after that, but he promised he would stop taking the pills. I believed him, because I still believed in him. He was still taking pills though.

He soon dropped out of school. I told him he had to get his GED and enlist in the Army. He did and passed his ASFAB test with flying colors. His excitement for enlisting soon changed and he began to avoid his recruiters. He told me he was afraid. I was afraid too. I was lost at this point. What can I do to help my son? His life was taking a turn for the worse. Why was he doing this to himself? He was so smart, handsome, and loved by so many. I was confused and scared for his future. But what else could I do?

One night though, I got my chance to intervene. He came home under the influence of who knows what. It really freaked me out. I jumped in my car and drove up to the police station; they followed me back to the house and arrested him. They put him in juvenile detention for 10 days. He was court ordered to house arrest and mandatory drug and alcohol treatment. Finally, I thought this was going to be his chance to get his life back. After ten days the house arrest was over. He started to drink again, I threatened to call his PO but I never did.

My son went out that afternoon and came home drunk. I was so upset I did not speak to him that evening. That night after I was in bed, he came in my room and asked if he could spend the night at his friend's house. I asked him, "Aren't you suppose to start a new job in the morning?" He said "don't worry Mom, I will get a ride and when I get off work I will mow the lawn." I said OK, told him I loved him. He replied I love you too.

Those are the last words I ever heard my son say to me. Around 4:30 that morning RJ came home. I never heard him though. I woke up about 7 to take the dog out. As I came down the steps I saw him. Face down on the floor, the computer chair next to him was on its side. I rolled him over and instantly I knew something was terribly wrong. I called 911, the dispatcher told me to give him CPR. I did not know how, but I did anyways. My baby boy needed me. When the paramedics arrived they had to pull me off of him. Everything was happening so fast. The police started to question me but I did not have the answers. They put him in the ambulance, and I followed close behind. I could not understand why the sirens and lights were not on and why they were not rushing him to the hospital. Now I understand why. When I arrived I threw the insurance card to the ER receptionist. They put me in a room and shortly after, the doctor came in. He told me my son was unresponsive and that they have tried everything. If they kept trying to get him back there would be a huge chance he would never be the same. No matter how badly I wanted him here with me I could not do that to him. My son used to love, laugh and live. He would never be himself again. I told them to stop trying. I still regret that choice to this day. I will never know if I made the right choice, I will never know if he would have ever been the same boy I knew and loved so deeply.

119

My son lost his life to a mixture of alcohol, Xanax and Suboxone. On his death certificate it says "Adverse Reaction to drugs" It should have read "cause of death overdose." The mixture slowed his breathing and his heart stopped. My son was one in a million, but in 2008 he was one in 15,000 who died as a result of prescription pills and the numbers go up every year.

My son did what the other teenagers did that night, but my son came home and never woke up. Teenagers do not realize that drinking with friends can quickly turn into taking pills and addiction. In the suburbs of PA where I am from, this problem is rising every day. To the kids they see the pills as a prescription and not hard drugs like cocaine or heroin, so it cannot hurt them. My son thought the same thing.

There is not a day that goes by that I do not cry for him. He died 6 weeks after I had him put in jail to try to help him. His probation officer never set up his drug and alcohol classes. My son did not get to drive, he will never turn 18, and he did not go into the service or college. He never woke up to start his new job or get to come home to mow the lawn. He will be 17 forever. I miss him more than anything in this world. My job, house or anything else in life is no longer important. Those are just things. All the things I used to yell about, like his messy room, beard trimmings on the sink or clothes left in the dryer, I wish I had back. I am reminded of RJ every day, either from a song on the radio, something in a movie, or something I hear someone say. All the things that made up my son and the person that he was, is just a memory now.

Instead of my son starting his senior year or me buying him a car for his 18th birthday, I bought him a headstone. I live with the guilt every day, questioning myself. Why didn't I hear my son come home that night? Why did I tell him he could go out? I should have called his PO officer when I had the chance. Why didn't I wake up sooner? If I did, would I have been able to save him?

I know I am unable to change the past, so I hope to educate for the future. I know my son would want to share his story and tell people it is not worth risking your life to take pills and drink alcohol. This will kill you; my son is proof of that.

RJs Mom

Jacki Smiro

The Struggles

Anyone who has witnessed firsthand an alcoholic's life knows it is the pit of hell. What you may not know though, is the personal struggles an alcoholic goes through. The debate they have with themselves to drink or not drink. You may have seen firsthand the torment and self-destruction that goes with being an alcoholic, but you may not know how many near death experiences an alcoholic has had. Their life is filled with danger and personal devastation. The internal damage that has been done normally cannot be reversed and can be fatal. Their liver becomes damaged, causing cirrhosis and alcohol induced hepatitis C. Their kidneys become damaged causing them to not contract properly which causes the body to lose blood supply. Their risk of having a heart attack and stroke intensifies each day they consume. Externally their skin turns yellow and is covered with open sores. Their capillary veins break in their face, especially their nose, due to an exceeded amount of alcohol going through their circulatory system. You may not know the blackouts they experience and the pain they are actually going through. An alcoholic may begin to hallucinate and think things are happening that are not, because the alcohol has corrupted their brain functioning. You may see they forget who you are and act confused, like a person struggling with Alzheimer's. The emotional distress and severe depression they feel due to their lack of self-worth and sadness weighs on them heavily. You may not understand they cannot eat because the alcohol has bloated their stomach, deteriorated their stomach lining and has created painful ulcers. You may know they get lost, confused and fall to the ground causing painful bruises, scratches and even broken bones. You may watch them stumble and sway back and forth trying to regain their balance. You may hear them scream out at night in fear and in anger due to the night terrors the alcohol has caused. You may watch them guzzle and indulge themselves in their alcohol to drown their bodies out of their reality. You may hear them cry and sob about the things they have done and the things they feel they cannot change. You may hear them slur their words and mumble under their breath. You may not know they daydream and fantasize about being sober, but fear if they do they will die and if they don't they will also die. You may watch them frantically search for the hidden bottles they have stored away for themselves. When they can't find them or realize they already drank them, they get angry, because they know they will soon experience the gut wrenching pains from the withdrawal. You know how bad they are hurting themselves physically and mentally, and you know it is out of your control. You also know that what this addiction has turned them into is not who they once were and not who they want to be.

You know the ugly, sad, and terrifying truth about what alcohol can do. I know I do, I watched it first hand and you have too.

"My dad was not born into addiction, nor did he wake up one day and say hey, today is the day I am going to be an alcoholic and throw my life away"

<u>The feeling</u>

February 22nd the moment I experienced in the bathroom doorway is the very moment I believe Jesus sent his angels down to save my dad from his addiction. The phone call I received at work was my brother in law calling to tell me him and my mom had found my dad.

I believe Jesus wanted me to feel his passing that day, for me to know that all his stress and worries have been lifted and to give me a sense of reassurance that everything was truly going to be alright. The Heavens had watched my dad struggle long enough and knew he did not deserve this life style; the life of a person dying from their addiction. Jesus knew his heart and knew this was not the man he was. He knew he was better than this and deserved eternal life with no worries, no addiction, and no stress.

That is the ironic feeling of hope I felt the day he passed on. I was devastated by his passing, but deep in my heart I knew he was in a much better place, and happier than he ever was.

"I will always remember your voice,

I understand Heaven was your choice

The day the angels came,

My life has never been the same

I know everything I was taught,

I now understand this addiction you fought.

I can still feel your love,

Coming down from Heaven up above.

I will always remember your laughter,

I know in my heart you are happily ever after."

<u>Remembering</u>

What I have realized is that this is not the legacy we want for our loved ones. My dad's legacy is not of an alcoholic who lost his life to his addiction. He was much better than that. Before there was this sickness called addiction that stole away our lives and the lives of our loved ones, there was a life that we celebrated. A life that we happily talked about and shared fun memories about. A life that God had created for us to love and cherish. That's the life I want to remember. Not the times when I had to rescue my dad head down in a hot tub inches away from the water, or hear and watch him cry because he thought he had nothing else worth living for, or the time I had to rush him to the emergency room while I saw the terror in his eyes and listened to the sadness in his voice as he held on to his life that he had given up on. I do not want to remember the time the paramedics had to wheel him out of his own home on a stretcher, because at that very moment we thought the alcohol had won. Or watching him stumble, run into walls and fall after guzzling down a 5th of vodka. The phone calls we would have, listening to his sad heart wanting to be different, but not knowing how or where to start. Praying with him for strength and knowledge to lead him in the right direction. Those are the memories I try to block out. I want you to block your bad memories out too. Trust me; your loved one that lost their life to addiction or has recovered does not want to be remembered by all their bad times. I am sure there are so many good and funny memories that if you think hard enough you can quickly replace all the bad memories that haunt you every day.

"Remembering the good memories of our loved ones may bring tears to our eyes; but these memories are what keep our loved ones alive"

"Dear Daddy,

There are so many things I wish I could have told you before it was your time. I forgave you and loved you when you were at your worst and your heart was weak. I never held you accountable in the end for what the addiction did to you.

I know now, the struggles you endured. I knew your heart and your soul; I knew you did not want this life. I knew how your pride and self-worth were so shot down from the hatefulness of society and how hard it was for you to see beyond the hurt and anger. I can surpass the anger and sadness I saw in you though, I can remember you when you were happy, always making jokes about everything, always being goofy, enjoying everything about life. Your smile brightened a dark room and your voice always made heads turn. I will always remember the funny dances you would do and the way you would always sing Elvis Presley and Dean Martin songs. Showing off your muscles and doing the "peck dance" always made us laugh.

I will always remember the way you accepted us for who we were and even though you did not agree with some of our choices we made, you always respected them and supported us.

I will always remember your proud smile when all 5 of your grandchildren were born. You gave each one of them your love and affection like they were your very own kids. You took them on special walks, celebrated birthday parties with them, took them for ice cream, and wagon rides. You took time out of your days to have special phone calls with them and you made up funny nicknames that individualized each grandkid. They will always remember the good times you spent with them and they talk about you still as they grow older.

Everyone enjoyed being around you because you always had something funny to say or some interesting story. You taught me how to make the best peanut butter milkshakes that I will pass down to my kids and they will pass to theirs. I know you raised me to be a good person like you were raised and I have become that image of you. I am proud of the things you had accomplished in life. You too were always so proud of yourself when you had done something great, always wanting to show it off and teach others how to be proud of themselves too.

You taught me how to laugh and not to take things too seriously, especially when life got hard. I try to practice that kind of attitude every day. I choose to put a smile on my face every morning, no matter how I feel, because I know you would want me to. What the addiction did to you is unfair; I wish deeply we were more prepared for the road the alcohol took you down, the way it quickly stole you from us.

I went to war with your addiction and your addiction won. I live with the guilt of not being able to help you, but I know in my heart you would not want me to feel that way, so I have replaced that feeling with the feeling of hope and courage, that I can help other people help themselves. I know you would be proud of me for that.

You taught me how to care and be respectful of others. I

think of the things you taught me and the way I was raised every day, I try to teach and raise my kids like that as well. Even though I thought you were a little strict at times, I know now it was because you loved us so much and wanted the best for our futures.

I wish you had the knowledge of what the alcohol was going to do to you before it was too late, and had the resources to handle all the ups and downs that came into your life. I know I cannot change the past, therefore I hope to educate others about the severity of alcohol addiction and how to cope with life's downfalls.

When you passed, I prayed that you did not go to your grave with a sad heart; I prayed that you knew how much your family loved you and how much we cared about you. I prayed that you did not feel alone, that you held us in your heart with every last breath you took. I prayed that the angels wrapped you in their arms and hugged you tight telling you everything will be alright. I prayed that God opened his arms to you and forgave you of your sins and let you come into his Kingdom with all the pride and self-worth you deserved.

I believe strongly in what I prayed for. I have the confidence and faith that God took care of you that day.

Daddy, you are my inspiration, I loved you at your best and I loved you at your worst. You were such a strong person and even the strongest become weak. I promise you I will never become weak nor surrender my soul to addiction."

I love you, your daughter Kathy

"Forever I will remember
The day the angels came

Forever I will remember
They saved you from your pain

Forever I will remember
Your laugh and sweet smile

Forever I will remember
Life only last for a little while

Forever I will remember
The things that I was taught

Forever I will remember
The battle that you fought

Forever I will remember
Your strong pride and dignity

Forever I will remember
You will now be happy for eternity"

4

<u>Crystal Meth</u>

"Cold alone and broken, the only thing I can feel is the pain in my heart. I can hear the ones around me cry for me and try to help me, but I feel so ashamed of myself I cannot face them.

I have lost my touch with reality, I hear them but I ignore them and feed my pain with more drugs. A way of selfishness this is. I am so absorbed in feeling sorry for myself; I have no love or worry for anyone else. As long as I have my drug, I know no one can hurt me.

It is like there is a reality I am scared to accept. I used to be a normal person, doing everyday normal things. A person with real dreams and ambitions. This drug has kidnapped my sanity and taken my very existence away. I try to get it back but I cannot seem to see beyond my hurt. I wish there was a quick fix, but I know the road ahead is going to be the hardest thing I have ever done. The road to recovery. I am very scared. I pray I will make it there one day."

Meth facts and history

Crystal meth is a highly addictive stimulant that is very toxic to the body. It is very similar to amphetamine. On the streets it can be known as meth, chalk, ice, crystal, speed, crank, the shit, and glass.

Crystal meth is not a new street drug; this drug has been around since the early 1900s. Meth was administered in WWII to keep soldiers in fighting mode. Adolf Hitler and his followers were highly addicted to crystal meth. In Japan it was given as a "work pill" to produce energy and rid fatigue in the workers. It was not until late 1960 that people started to realize that this drug had dangerous side effects and was a major health threat (Crystal Meth Addiction, 2002-2012).

Meth ingredients, usage and smell

Have you ever looked around your house and noticed all the chemicals you have? You may not, but a crystal meth addict will. Crystal meth can be made by almost anything from your household products or things around the garage. It can be snorted, taken orally, injected with a needle, or heated and smoked.

Here is a list of some crystal meth ingredients and the things you may need to cook this drug.

- Acetone
- Rubbing alcohol
- Anhydrous ammonia
- Battery acid
- Benzene
- Camera batteries
- Camp stove fuel
- Chloroform
- Cold tablets
- Diet pills
- Drain cleaner
- Energy boosters
- Ephedrine
- Starting fluid
- Freon
  - Gasoline additives
  - Iodine crystals

- Lithium batteries

- Hydrochloric acid

- Muriatic acid

- Paint thinner

- Iodine

- Phenyl acetone

- Phenylpropanolamine

- Pheynl-2-propane

- Propane cylinders

- Red devil lye

- Red phosphorous

- Rock, table, or Epsom salt

- Sodium metal

- Stained coffee filters

- Toluene

- Tubing

- White gasoline

- Wooden matches

(Crystal Meth Addiction. 2002-2012)

Due to the rise of meth labs, many retailers have removed ephedrine and pseudo ephedrine medicines and put them behind the counter to help control the amount sold. You now must show I.D to buy these products. Ephedrine is a popular known ingredient in meth.

When an addict smokes crystal meth, it smells soft and a little sweet. The average person most likely will not be able to detect what this smell is, but an experienced user will. When an addict is a heavy user, they have a very strange odor that comes off them, almost chemical smelling like ammonia and cat urine, very hard to explain, but definitely not a familiar smell.

<u>Signs and effects of a meth user</u>

Crystal meth addicts are easily recognized among other drug and alcohol users. The signs of a meth addict can be:

- Rapid eye movement and dilated pupils
- Low body weight
- Appear to be sick
- Major dental problems, severe tooth decay and softening of the teeth
- Open skin sores, users often pick at imaginary bugs they believe are under their skin called "crystal meth bugs"
- Strange body odor
- Faces of addicts are often sunken in, cheek bones showing, pale splotchy, and may be sweaty and oily looking
- They may have ticks and twitch from long term use
- They may wear sunglasses to hide their eyes
- They may also disappear for days and weeks at a time while using

The effects of crystal meth can last up to 12 hours, causing a rush of euphoria and energy. When an addict is withdrawing from meth it can take days up to weeks to rid the body of the drug.

Crystal meth addicts are the most dangerous addicts to be

around or confront. Due to their delusional thoughts, lack of sleep, agitation, and mood swings, especially while being in the tweaker stage (when an addict has not slept for days or weeks). A crystal meth addict can be very unpredictable and may lash out at any moment. They can be very violent and since they already feel paranoid, confronting them can have negative consequences

.   When someone overdoses on meth it happens unexpectedly and suddenly.

Signs of meth overdose can include:

- Heart attack
- Coma
- Convulsions
- Cardiovascular collapse
- High fever
- Sweating
- Stroke
- Death

(Crystal Meth Addiction, 2002-2012)

Crystal meth has short term effects and long term effects on its users.

Short term effects can include:

- Increased wakefulness
- Decreased appetite
- Increased respiration
- Increased physical activity
- Hypothermia
- Increased heart rate and blood pressure
- Irregular heart beat
- Insomnia
- Cardiovascular collapse
- Irritability
- Confusion
- Anxiety

Long term effects from meth can include:

- Hallucinations
- Violent and aggressive behavior
- Schizophrenia
- Possible brain damage
- Anxiety
- Depression
- Lowered immunity
- Poor coping skills

The High

"I want you to take a deep breath....... clear your mind of all your thoughts and put yourself in the shoes of this addict...................

  You're in a cold dark room by yourself, curtains closed, with no light coming in. The world around you is quiet and still. You feel paranoid, so you check again to see if the doors are locked. You make sure the curtains are covering any peep holes in the window. You check under the bed and in the closet to make sure no one is hiding in there. You already know you're going to regret what you're about to do, but you feel if you don't, you will start to feel anxious and unsteady. A feeling you hate to feel. You debate with yourself not to use, but quickly your drug defeats your mind. Your heart aches and your body feels destroyed. You're dehydrated, hungry and have not slept for days. As your stomach growls, you ignore it as you rub your burning eyes. The air you breathe in around you smells of stale smoke. You can smell your body odor and dirty hair, you try to remember the last time you showered or even left your room, but you cannot. You can taste the dirty grime in your mouth and feel the slime and crust on your teeth. Your tongue feels so dry and your gums have sores all over them from chewing your mouth nervously.

  As you stare at yourself in the mirror, the image of how you thought you looked has faded away and the real image is coming clear. Your beautiful face is now sunken in and covered with sores. Your eyes are glazed over and dark. Your cheeks remind you of an old Indian woman. You start to remember how you used to look, pretty and healthy with a nice glow to your skin, your face was clear and your eyes and cheeks were not sunken in. That image seems so long ago. You also notice your arms, how skinny they are and any muscle you once had is now gone. Your skin is pale and you are malnourished. The drugs are quickly eating your very existence away, internally and externally.

The past few days have all seemed to run together and your thoughts are hazed. After confirming you're alone and no one is going to interrupt you, you find yourself crouched over in a corner trying to hide from the world, but you question yourself how long you have been sitting there staring at the door handle to see if it is going to move. You pull out the bag that you believe holds your life. Pulling each item out, placing them in front of you as if it were gold. You stare at the needle closely debating with yourself if the brown spot on the tip is an illusion or someone else's blood stain. You try to remember where you got the needle, but cannot. It looks dirty and used to you, but it is the only one you have and there is no way of getting another one. You continue to stare blankly at the needle like it's going to magically become clean. It does not change so you decide to use it anyway, not caring if it is dirty and contaminated. You reassure yourself that it is not dirty and even if it was, who cares, you have already lost everything, what's one more downfall in your life. AIDS? Hepatitis C? You precisely prepare the rubber band around your arm. Tying it so tight your skin wrinkles. You push and feel softly on your skin trying to find the perfect vein, slowly running your fingers over the bruises and sores from your previous days. You find the vein that will soon be your victim. You close your eyes as the band around your arm holds your skin tight turning it red. As you pierce your skin, you feel the familiar comforting pain as the needle enters your body. Your blood quickly rushes inside the needle mixing with your drug like a volcano erupting. You hold your hand steady as you push the needle in deeper to the middle of your vein. The core of your soul. This needle is filled with the only substance that you believe makes you feel alive. As you slowly inject yourself, the rush begins. You feel the burn go through your veins; you close your eyes and squeeze your free hand tight, clinching it like you're holding onto your last bit of hope. Your body feels like it's lifting up and away from the floor, the reality you're in instantly goes away as your mind drifts off into a euphoric state. Every inch of your body feels so tingly it's almost numb. You clinch your jaw tight pressing your teeth so hard against each other they fill like they could crack. Your eyes start to roll a little to the back of your head and you feel as if you're floating. Your heart starts to pound so hard, you think you can see your chest move. Every pain you've ever imagined has disappeared now and you are left with no worries in the world. You release the rubber band from your arm, leaving the needle in place in hopes every last drop will be absorbed. You sit, soaking up this feeling, trying to embrace it with full force because you know it will not last.

Not knowing how much time has passed, you are now

sprawled out on the floor on your back, arms and legs stretched out around you. Staring at the ceiling you still feel the rush storming through your body. Quickly your body is indulged with energy and you feel you have become alive again. You feel that you can conquer the world and defeat anything. So many thoughts are racing through your mind, so you grab your journal and pen that was a few feet away from you. You begin scribbling your rambling thoughts down on paper so vigorously you cannot read your own hand writing. You're writing about folk tales you knew as a child, then about the boy you once had a crush on, now both memories are mixed together and you have created a fictional story. You imagine you're in this fairytale of a world. You have created a new life for yourself. You create a beautiful world full of colorful flowers and dancing kitty cats. You see yourself flying in the sky with the birds. You start to illustrate your story with those flowers and birds. In your mind you see them so pretty, but as you look again at your paper you see black scribbles and words you can make out. As you stare at your paper, your imaginary place is forgotten. You get a sudden feeling of fear, a dark shadow flashes in your eyes. Your tingly feeling is slowly leaving your body. You can start to feel the aches in your muscles. You notice the needle still stuck in your arm, blood now dripping down to your fingertips. You feel almost claustrophobic as you gasp for deep breaths. Another dark shadow seems to cover your eyes. You start to see and feel the demons all around. The worst is about to happen.

Your high quickly comes to an end. You grab the needle out of your arm, frantically searching for your bag so you can refill. Your mind is racing and your hands are trembling. You struggle as you maintain your composure long enough so you can liquefy your drug and suck it back into your needle. This time you try to use more, to reach that same high. You become more nervous and anxious, filling the needle up for the second time. Your body cannot experience the effects it had earlier, so you use more, and more, pushing the needle in harder, thinking it will penetrate deeper, allowing your body to soak up every last drop. Your mind is in a haze as you start to remember where you are; all of a sudden you're reminded it's only you and your drug. You're all alone, feeling scared and neglected. Reality is setting in, you see your life flash in your eyes, your mind is starting to race and your eyes are moving back and forth rigorously. You can see in your thoughts the friends you once had and the laughter y'all once shared. The children you once loved, cherished, and embraced with open arms. The home you had created, and devoted your life to. The love your heart once felt, but now so desperately aches for. As you're reminded of the things you have lost, you become upset, feeling sorry for yourself, wanting so badly to feel good again so you use more, this time more aggressively, you think if you keep using more your high will get better and you can soon forget all your worries. As you sit, just yourself and your drug, you are reminded once again what you gave up. You're mad and upset because your drug has let you down and you cannot feel the rush and euphoria like before. You now have become your drug, and your drug has become you. It has stolen everything from you. It is the only thing you depend on to make you feel good, but it is the one thing that has taking everything from you. Now you are stuck with a feeling of no way out. The only thing you know and have now is your drug, and now your drug can't even make you feel good anymore. All your hopes and dreams seem so far away, even though they could be so close if you let them. You are praying hard inside that someone will come to your rescue, but do you really want the rescue? No, because then you will have to face all your fears, all the fears you have been suppressing for so long with your drug, all the people you have betrayed and let down. You feel weak and tormented by the life you are now living. The guilt you feel makes you so sick you start to gag, wanting so badly to throw it all up. The fear, the sadness, the anger, but all that comes out is burning stomach acid. You know that the only person that can save you from this is yourself. You tell yourself to dig deep inside your soul and find yourself, the person you were before the drugs. You try to see and feel those happy memories you forgot and the love you once felt. You try to visualize your life before the drugs and the chaos. Your memories remind you that there is hope still there. You do know what love is because you were once surrounded by its beauty. Now you tell yourself it is time to be strong and fight the war against your addiction. You want so badly for someone to tell you they love you and support you through this. You know becoming sober will be scarier than the first time you used, but in your heart you can feel the strength you have within, so you get on your knees and pray, asking God to give you the strength to overcome this addiction, praying for His love to guide you down the right path. You now surrender yourself to Him instead of your drug. You cry out to Him with open arms. You wish you could feel wet tears streaming down your face, but your emotions have been depleted for so long your eyes remain dry. You want so badly to sob out of control and let it all out, but you cannot. You beg God to accept you for who you really are. You scream so loudly at Him, almost like you're mad at the One that gave you life and the One that loves you unconditionally. Whimpering as you slowly come back to your reality, you lower your hands to your sides and bow your head down as you pray for forgiveness.

At this point, you look around you as you come back to the dark, stale room you have been hiding in for so long, this room where you just spent the last 24 hours. You feel confused, hopeful, scared, but driven. It is now time to surrender yourself to God and let Him lead the way."

5

<u>Recovery is Possible</u>

There is hope

"You are not fully alive if you live in fear of change"

Recovery is possible for those who really want it. Although not every addict will be able to live through their addiction to tell their recovery story, there is still hope out there. God provides us with the strength to move on, but it is up to them to find that strength.

People often ask me how I became an addict. My answer was simple; things are not always what they seemed. Many would look at me puzzled and they had good reason. I was viewed as the woman who had the perfect life. I had the big house, loving husband, beautiful children, sports car, fashionable clothes, accessories, name brand purses, and many diamonds. What they could not see was what was inside of me; my inner pain and anger. My life as a child was broken. I grew up around men who tormented me and abused me. My mother did not know how to love me and often turned her back on me. I carried all these emotions with me as I grew older. My scarred heart did not know what love was. I went through many bad relationships with older men in search of someone to take care of me. The one thing I did know was how to carry myself. I always looked sophisticated and rich, even when I was not. This attracted a lot of men with money to me. They often treated me more like an escort than the fancy rich girl I was trying to be. This hurt me emotionally more then I knew how to handle. It all stopped though when I met my husband. He valued me like gold. I finally felt complete and thought my life was finally making sense. My husband did not know about my past and with his high profile job and reputation I could not let him know my inner torment. Our life together started out great and I thought I had forgotten all about my past. I was wrong. My husband worked very long hours which left me alone with our kids. The stress of that and being alone started to bring back all those childhood memories. I tried to block them out but could not. I did not have any close friends or family to talk to, so I did the next thing I knew. I started by taking a few shots at night to knock me out. My husband would get home late so he never knew what I was doing. During my days, I was feeling more depressed and I realized that all the materialistic things in my life were not making me feel loved or happy like I thought they would. I wanted more than anything in the world to feel happy and to feel love. That is when the drinking really began. My husband was rarely home at this point, his job demanding a lot of his time. My daytime drinking started with a few shots throughout the day to help relieve my tension with the kids and me feeling alone. I was able to hide this from the people around me so well no one expected anything was wrong. I turned into a functioning alcoholic. The more I drank though, the sadder I felt. The memories I was trying to block out seemed to haunt me even more. I would have flashbacks in my sleep or alcohol induced hallucinations during the day. Many times I would lock myself in my bedroom and drink all day while my kids (under the age of 5) ran around the house fending for themselves. Having a lot of money allowed my drinking to progress quickly. I realized I could pay our nanny more money to watch the kids all day and half the night with no questions asked. Of course doing this, I was not being a mother to them; I was being a selfish drunk. No one really noticed though, I was wealthy and it was not uncommon for wealthy mothers to have their kids with their nannies. I think by this time though, my husband knew something was wrong, but he did not have the time to address it. He was in and out of the house quickly. We rarely talked and if we did it was an argument over something. Two years into my addiction to alcohol I was in full force. My life had already begun to spiral out of control, but I could not see it because I was too drunk. I was drunk from the time I woke up, to the time I passed out. I was so self-absorbed with my drinking, I was oblivious to the world around me. My nanny now watched my kid's full time and my husband had nothing to do with me when he was home. Everything in my life was a blur. I do not even remember the day my husband took our kids and moved out. He left me alone with money and a house, all bills paid. I drank myself into a coma a few months after they left. The maid who came to clean found me on the bathroom floor, naked, laying in my throw up. I spent a week in the hospital. When I was released, I felt somewhat level headed. I realized what I had lost and felt more alone than ever. I was once the beautiful and respected wife of a brain surgeon, I had a family that loved me, but I did not see it. I knew at that point I needed help. I reached out to my estranged husband, not to get him back, but for resources. He helped me find a treatment center and supported me throughout my recovery. In my recovery I learned that materialistic things, money, nor alcohol would make me feel happy, feel loved or take away my problems. I learned to embrace my past and forgive the ones who hurt me. In doing so, I was able to move on and leave all that sadness and anger behind me. My life is not perfect, but I have learned to live sober, love myself, my kids, and my life for what it is. When people ask me how someone like me could have become an addict I tell them God had a plan for my future, but he just had to challenge me first.

I now help those who are lost, just like I once was.

Rebecca Smith

For an addict using, there is nothing worse than knowing you need help, asking for it, and then hiding from the people who have offered help because you haven't followed their advice. The recovering addicts who have made suggestions know you disappeared because you messed up, but they also have compassion because they know the shame and guilt you're torturing yourself with. Do yourself a favor - call them and fess up. There's no shame in struggle. We were all there once, keep trying.

Patty Powers-Sober Coach

Pattypowersnyc.com

I spent all my 20's and half my 30's in a blur of confusion and pure madness. I was addicted to Crystal Meth.

I lost everything and everyone I had ever cared about. The only thing I cared about was when, where and how I was going to get my next fix.

The word "life" meant nothing to me, I could breathe, but I felt nonexistent. My mind, body and soul was controlled by my addiction. There were many times during my addiction that I could not afford my drug. I was desperate to get my fix, so I turned to the streets for help. I indulged myself in the dirtiest deeds for men and even women in exchange for drugs. In this part of my addiction I did not care about morals or diseases. I just needed my drug.

Every day I had a debate with myself. I did not want to live, but I didn't want to die either. I would ask myself "what did I have to live for?" When I could not think of an answer, I would ask myself who would miss me if I died? And if death was my next step,

how would I make that happen? I never had any answers for my
questions, so the debate went on in my head every day. I felt this
personal debate was the only thing keeping me alive.

In my many years of addiction I did try to quit many times.
I tried to stay away from the drugs and keep to myself. Trying to
fight my temptations alone was hard. Every time I tried to quit, I
failed and went right back into the lifestyle I knew I would regret.
I finally accepted the fact that this was my lifestyle and nothing
more. I would be an addict for the rest of my life.

When my family and friends would reach out and help me, I
felt like a charity case to them. I also felt like they did not
understand my struggles and how hard it was for me to quit. My
life was full of panic, confusion and pure madness
I felt very singled out and alone. I think all I wanted to hear was
for someone to tell me everything was going to be alright and that
they still had faith in me. Even if someone had told me that, I
would not have changed at that time, but I believe those words
would have given me hope.

The longer and the more I used, the worse I felt. My life
revolved around 2 options: To die miserably, feeling sorry for
myself, high on crystal meth or to seek help.

After years of drug use, suicidal thoughts and rage, I finally
made the choice to save myself. I did not know how, but I knew if I
really set my heart in the right direction, I could do it. First I made
a promise to myself that I could never go back on. I knew at this

point it was life or death for me. I started out calling rehabs and halfway houses. I found one that would help me financially until I found a job and could afford my house fees.

This was the biggest thing I had done for myself in my entire life. I signed into the halfway house feeling scared, hopeful and still high. My journey into recovery had begun. Everything I had secretly wished for had come true and I was the one who made it all happen. No one did it for me. I was in control of my future and it felt so good.

I would be lying if I said recovery was easy. It has definitely been the hardest thing I have done, but the fact that I am doing it and enjoying it, I would not change it for anything. To feel real feelings and to finally have the tools and knowledge to work throughout life's challenges is rewarding. Knowing I can live my life sober gives me strength to challenge myself. I went from living on the streets trading sex for drugs, to earning my high school diploma and now looking into college.

I look back at my life and the things I went through as a child and young adult with closure. The only thing that haunts me now is knowing if I had the tools and knowledge back then, I would have never chosen drugs to escape from my problems.

I have celebrated sobriety everyday with pride and dignity since 2007. My motto is, I used to chase drugs, now I chase my dreams

Recovered drug addict

Valerie Meza

Being sober is the best gift I could have ever given myself

and my family. The biggest step in my recovery was admitting to the ones I had hurt the worst and owning up to my actions. I asked for forgiveness from them and they granted it. At that moment I realized how precious and important family is.
Recovered alcoholic
Aaron Jenkins

After countless downfalls while trying to stay and get sober on my own I finally realized that my problems ran deeper than just my addiction. I thought I could just forget about it all and move on, but I was being haunted every day. I did not think treatment and counseling was right for me, but what was wrong for me was not treating myself. After entering treatment I was nervous, but I knew I had to in order to relieve myself of my personal torment. I needed to learn life again and how to take care of myself. I thought people would look down on me and judge me for this decision, but they actually praised me for it. I had to leave my old life behind in order to move on and that also meant leaving behind my family for a bit. They knew though I was sick and in order for me to be there for them I had to first be there for myself........
Recovered crystal meth addict
Sherri Long

"Addiction does not define who you are; it is just part of your journey in finding yourself"

157

Tattoo

The pain getting my tattoo was excruciating. Imagine hours and hours with many sessions, with needles being scraped into your back. This pain though I believe, could not be compared to the pain that an addict must feel internally.

I tried to put myself in the shoes of a suffering addict while getting my tattoo, trying to see how well I could ignore the pain without taking any internal drugs. It was very hard. If I had something to take the pain away, it would have made it much easier. I think this is how most addicts feel. They just want to take the pain away, even if it is for a moment.

Realistically the pain an addict is trying to make go away does not. It is just numb for a while, just like numbing gel does for a tattoo. It relieves the skin for a bit like drugs/alcohol may relieve an addict for a short amount of time. But the pain comes back and it's normally worse than before. Skin being tattooed becomes red, bloody and very sore. The longer the tattoo session, the worse it gets. The numbing gel wears off very quickly leaving the pain almost unbearable, just like when an addict is coming down. Their pain is still there, but intensified now because not only do they have the pain they started out with, they now have the pain of coming off the drugs/alcohol.

After a tattoo session your skin is an open wound. You have to nurture it with lotions and antibacterial soaps to make sure it does not get infected, also like an addict has to do when they are coming down. Their internal emotions are very open like a wound. They have to guard and nurture themselves to become strong. If they are unable to do so, infection can set in. The addict's infection though is their need to get high or drunk.

I chose my back to put this tattoo because it is the backbone of your body, the strongest part. Your back carries you and supports you. It is your outer strength.

When I was 16 my dad gave me a cross necklace. This necklace means the world to me and I have never taken it off. The cross on my tattoo is that cross, except in my tattoo it has one diamond shining in the middle to represent my dad. The necklace itself has diamonds all throughout it.

The heart around the cross is made up of ginger flowers. The ginger flowers represent pride. For my tattoo represents that no matter what happened in my dad's life, I will be forever proud of him and love him unconditionally.

The sunrise is heaven and all its glory; I believe that is where my dad is.

The doves represent peace and tranquility.

The verse that is in the scroll reads:

When I called you answered me, you made me bold by strengthening my soul. Psalms 138:3

In the beginning I was weak; I prayed to Jesus one night to give me the strength I needed to go on. I believe Jesus heard me loud and clear that night. I have never felt so courageous and free from fear since then.

The cherry blossoms represent his beautiful life. Cherry blossoms do not bloom very long, but when they do they are beautiful and unique, just like life. I have the cherry blossoms growing up into the sunrise to show that even though life was not beautiful all the time for him on earth, it will be beautiful for him now in Heaven.

Finding Faith and Prayer

"Forgiving yourself is the biggest step in believing yourself "

I believe prayer has a big impact if you are a believer, but you have to believe in what you are praying for.

Do not be like the waves in the ocean that go the way the wind blows, believe in what you ask your Father in Heaven and be strong in faith. Faith is what we hope for but do not see, so be thankful in the knowledge that God is listening and wants you to trust in Him, not what things appear.

I received that text from my friend in a moment when I needed some hope.

I believe we are given the obstacles in our life for a reason. God knew our paths when we were created, but it is up to us on how we act upon them. It is like a test of our faith and strength to prove we can overcome what has been given to us. I also believe that God will not put situations in our life we cannot handle; even if they end in "tragedy", it happened for a reason. May it be a lesson we learned, or an example used to save another life.

Fear not for I am with you; be not dismayed, for I am your God; I

will strengthen you, I will help you, I will uphold you with my

righteous right hand.

Isaiah 41:10 NKJV

I believe He chose my dad to show and teach others that if you do not get a hold of your addiction and change your life, it will result in death. I believe He chose me to show and teach others that a person cannot save or change someone if they are not ready or are in denial.

Rejoice in our suffering, suffering produces perseverance,

perseverance character and character hope.

Romans 5:3-4 NIV

Whenever you're struggling or scared, be open with the Man upstairs, He will listen, and He hears your heart. He has made the path in your life and knows the struggles you will endure. God believes in you, therefore you should believe in yourself.

"In the name of Jesus Christ, I pray.

Dear Lord,

Please guide me through these hard times. In these troubling times I am filled with fear and sadness. I reach my hand out to you, and ask that you walk beside me. I cannot carry all my burdens, but I know you can and will. Please walk beside me. Please guide me. Please help me hold on strong through the trials and the storms. Help me hold onto my faith in the darkest hour. Stay with me Lord, and show me Your way. In Your love and Holy Spirit I abide.

Amen."

Within 7 years addiction took my dad's life on February 22nd, 26 days after he entered the treatment center to try to get help. He was only 50 years old. I am grateful, in a way; he had those few days in the end of being sober. Even though he did not feel good, it was good to see him that way.

I enjoyed the breakfast I got to bring him and the small talks we had. I believe God knew what he was doing. He gave me those few moments in the end for me to remember him for who he was. I will never take that for granted.

6

Authors Note

Life is like a puzzle,

At first the pieces are scattered out all around you with unorganized confusion. You slowly start to create the outline of the puzzle as your guide. The outline creates your boundaries and securities. Now you need to fill the inner part of the puzzle; your life. You find a matching piece right away. It was such a relief, but then you look at the other hundreds of pieces lying there hopelessly.

You pick up another piece, inspecting its outer shape and the colors that make up its design. You try to place it but cannot find its fit. As you encounter many frustrations and stress, you start to feel defeated by this one puzzle piece. Putting that piece down for a while you grab another, finding the perfect fit almost right away. Avoiding the pieces that you know will cause you stress, you try to pick out the obvious fitting ones first. As you put the puzzle together, you start to feel anxious because you know you will soon have to find the fit to the harder pieces. You take a break, sit back and stare at what you have accomplished so far, amazed with yourself for all your hard work. You pick up the one piece that you gave up on earlier; struggling with this piece you start to question yourself, why can't I find the right fit? Should I just give up and be done with the puzzle? Is this puzzle even worth all this work? You stare at the piece then at the puzzle. Feeling overwhelmed, you try to force the piece to fit. No luck. Getting frustrated with yourself and the puzzle piece you put it down once again, picking up an easier fitting piece. This piece fits perfectly. As time passes, the puzzle is almost complete. Even though it is starting to look beautiful you have experienced frustrations, stress, and anxiety. You felt defeated and even thought about giving up at one point. You look again at the one piece that has been giving you so much trouble; again you pick it up staring at it, trying to figure out the shape and colors. You stare blindly at the almost completed puzzle. Then all of a sudden you see it, the perfect fit. You have defeated the one piece you almost gave up on. All it took was a little hard work, patience and not giving up, for the other pieces to fill in for the hard piece to fit. Finally, your beautiful puzzle is complete.

What I am trying to say is through our journey in life it will be beautiful, hard and stressful. All the pieces may not come together perfectly or at one time, but with patience and never giving up, in the end it will all come together, creating something so beautiful it was all worth it.

Contacts

Ontheoutsidelookingin.net

Patty Peters- Steppingintochange.com

Patty Powers- Pattypowersnyc.com

Counseling for those effected by alcohol addiction

1-888-425-2666 Al-anon.alateen.org

Alcohol Addiction resources 1-800-559-9503 Alcoholaddiction.org

Suicide Hot line 1-800-273-8255

Suicidepreventionlifeline.org

Intervention Services Inc. 1-800-995-9729

Interventionservicesinc.com

Crystal Meth Addiction 1-866-596-1990 Crystalmethaddiction.org

References

Alcohol in America. (2005, April 4). Oracle think quest. Retrieved March 20, 2012, from http://library.thinkquest.org/04oct/00492/Alcohol_in_America.htm

Alcohol statistics. (2003-2012). Drug statistics. Retrieved March 10, 2012, from drug-statistics.com/alcohol.htm

Coon,N.L. (1998).Mosby's Dictionary Fifth addition: Guide to common drug interactions. (pp.1895-1896). Addictive Personality. (p. 34). (pp.898,64,625,183,320,756,1541,1051,358,1022,484,1593,1465,81,1637,784,1022,1013,1331,1179,1368,1465,75,1231). Saint Louis, Missouri: Mosby's Inc.

Crystal Meth ingredients. (2002-2012). Crystal Meth addiction. Retrieved April 21, 2012, from Crystalmethaddiction.org

Crystal Meth overdose. (2002-2012). Crystal Meth addiction. Retrieved April 21, 2012, from Crystalmethaddiction.org

History of Crystal Meth. (2002-2012) Crystal Meth addiction. Retrieved May 2nd, 2012, from Crystalmethaddiction.org

History of legal drinking age. (1997-2012) Virginia Department of Alcoholic Beverage Control. Retrieved October 22, 2012, from http://abc.state.va.us/facts/legalage.html

Lee,D. (2007). The 3 basic types of Alcohol or Drug Users. Family Intervention Handbook. (p. 25)

Lee, D. (2007). The progression rate of Addiction. Family Intervention Handbook. Page 13. (p. 42)

Mifflin,H.(2002). Addiction. Dictionary.com. Retrieved November, 2, 2012, from http://dictionary.reference.com/browse/addiction

Oracle Think Quest. (April 4, 2005). Prohibition Laws. Retrieved March 21st, 2012.from http://library.thinkquest.org/04oct/00492/Alcohol_in_America.htm

Wikipedia.(2012) (N.D). Twenty First Amendment to the United States Constitution. Retrieved April, 15th, 2012, from http://en.wikipedia.org/wiki/Twentyfirst_Amendment_to_the_United_States_Constitution http://en.wikipedia.org/wiki/Twentyfirst_Amendment_to_the_United_States_Constitution

Bio

Kathy has always enjoyed writing poetry and short stories even as a child. She had her first poem published when she was 9 years old. She met her husband in 2000 and they were married in 2008. They are currently raising three beautiful children.

In her spare time she enjoys painting and showing her abstract and contemporary art. She likes to challenge herself to new things and expand her knowledge in history, culture and holistic healing.

Kathy began writing *On the Outside Looking In* a few years after her dad passed away in 2008. Her writing helped her with the healing process. During her years of living on the blind side of her dad's alcohol addiction, she often felt confused, lost and defeated. The more she began to open up and talk to people about addiction she realized she was not the only one struggling. She learned there are many people searching for answers and healing. That's when

On the Outside Looking In came to life. She wanted to write a book where everything a person was looking for coming from both sides of addiction would be available.

Kathy is also the author of the children's series, The Cann Family. Having a family of her own, she understands how hard it is to talk to kids about certain life struggles. The Cann Family's "D" series is a series of books that cover little life challenges that families may go through while growing up. The Cann Family come up with creative solutions to each of those challenges. Each book comes with a fun family project to help the families interact and continue to talk about the challenge. The books range from simple things like how to choose healthy desserts, to doing your daily chores and then on to more serious subjects like how to say no to drugs and coping with death.

This series helps families create stronger foundations by building trust and communication skills.

After Kathy published her first book she realized she wanted to help other authors get their books out into the world. That is when she launched Live Love Learn Books Publishing. She believes when people can share their stories through their writing it will reach the ones who need it most.

She also knows how hard it is for non-fiction writers to go through the process in trying to find a traditional publisher.

Adding to Kathy's writing and publishing she is a professional motivational speaker.

KathyCarniero.com

Made in the USA
Charleston, SC
27 June 2016